D0899694

Homemade Products with
Brand-Name Quality

Homemade Products with Brand-Name Quality

250 Money-Saving Mixes

Charlette Carollo

PELICAN PUBLISHING COMPANY

Gretna 2010

Library of Congress Cataloging-in-Publication Data

Carollo, Charlette.
  Homemade products with brand-name quality : 250 money-saving
mixes / by Charlette Carollo.
    p. cm.
  Includes index.
  ISBN 978-1-58980-751-8 (pbk. : alk. paper) 1. Cookery. 2. Low budget
cookery. I. Title.
  TX714.C3731588 2010
  641.5'52—dc22
                            2010007383

Printed in the United States of America

Published by Pelican Publishing Company, Inc.
1000 Burmaster Street, Gretna, Louisiana 70053

I wish to dedicate this book to my children:
Norman Charles, Lisa, Matthew, Charlie, Daniel, Michele,
Helen, and Mary Margaret O'Brien. I love you for all that you
are and for all that you hope to be. May your dreams come true
as mine have come to me with this book.

CONTENTS

INTRODUCTION

Are you tired of trying to figure out how you can save money at the grocery? Are you frustrated having to take items off your shopping list because of increased costs? Have you wondered why your grocery bills keep getting higher and higher while you are eating less?

The truth of the matter is this: It's not necessarily the food that has brought up the prices, but rather the costs of labor, packaging materials, transportation, marketing, and advertisements that come together to bring the products to you, the consumer. These hidden "throw away" expenses result in the extra charges you pay at the checkout. These are normal company expenses, and they are promptly tacked on to each and every purchase you make. Most of us do not realize this when we put the products in our carts and head for the checkout.

Let's just imagine coming home from an exhaustive trip from the supermarket with $50.00 worth of groceries and then turning around and throwing away $25.00 of it into the garbage can. Those empty boxes cost us $25.00. Now, think about it. We just bought $25.00 worth of trash! Yet, by easily making your own homemade products using common, ordinary ingredients and packaging materials, such as zip-type plastic bags, odd jars and bottles, aluminum foil, and cartons, you've taken control of the situation and put a stop to this outlandish waste.

Homemade Products with Brand-Name Quality is a cookbook with 250 easy-to-make, money-saving recipes that offers a solution to today's high food prices and to surviving tough times by building up a well-stocked food pantry. It will give you insight into a completely new world of basic homemade cooking that is both nutritious and wholesome, foods with no preservatives and no additives. The types of foods you know are best for your family, made right in your own home. Moreover, because you have complete control over how your products are prepared, you have virtually eliminated the fear of food tampering and contamination.

For those with food allergies or salt-restrictive diets, this unique cookbook is perfect for you. It offers basic mixes of foods you enjoy that can be altered to fit your family's dietary needs.

This book was compiled and written to save you time, too. One only needs to make products in bulk or into extra food packets and then store them for later use. What a convenience not having to drive across town to the supermarket for a dozen mouth-watering jelly doughnuts when you can make them fresh right at home. And for creating a well-stocked pantry, there's no quicker or cheaper way than to package your own products yourself. This book will even help you organize and develop an effective plan toward self-sufficiency, giving you and your family peace of mind and security in times of national emergency or personal family crisis.

Homemade Products with Brand-Name Quality awakens your creativeness to make appreciative gifts for family and friends, people whom you care enough about to give a part of your time and talent. What a lovely gesture to give a thoughtful neighbor an assortment of your individual homemade cereals packed in a large, colorful cereal bowl with a spoon tied to a gigantic red bow.

Even if you've never made homemade mixes before, you are in for a rewarding experience. This innovative cookbook focuses on homemade, quality mixes you make yourself of products you enjoy the most.

Why Store Food

It doesn't take much in these uncertain times to find a logical reason for maintaining a well-stocked pantry. Purchasing extra products when they are on sale will result in extra savings when used after the price returns to normal. Saving time and gas are also important especially when you don't have to drive to the supermarket to purchase the one item you forgot to pick up earlier.

Loss of job or income, death of the spouse, illness, or prolonged periods of confinement in the home or hospital can bring about unexpected hardships to a family, particularly when there is very little food in the home to sustain them for any length of time. It might be months before things improve and relief is in sight. Until then, how will the family survive without food?

Crop failures are another important issue. Farmers depend on the right weather conditions, expecting to harvest abundant crops with each planting. Quite often, we have seen uncontrollable pests, floods, and inclement weather conditions quickly wipe out hundreds of acres of prime farmland within a matter of hours. Valuable planting time, thousands of dollars, and weeks of backbreaking labor have suddenly produced nothing but barren ground.

Hurricanes, blizzards, earthquakes, late snow storms, and other natural catastrophes are unforseeable situations that affect heavily on the supply of food in this country, for it is in these disastrous circumstances that food is almost always unavailable due to power outages and closed (sometimes demolished) stores. The matter is worsened when major highways are completely cut off and all transportation in and out suddenly stops. Sometimes profiteers will find their way into a community, offering supplies at skyrocketed prices far beyond what anyone can afford. This is what happened during Hurricane Katrina in 2005. Food storage then would have been a valuable asset to counteract those stressful and emotional times and to help one's neighbors.

With a country as large as ours and the continual loss of farmlands to investors, we might expect that the central warehouses of some chain supermarkets are equipped with only about thirty days supply of food for distribution to their store outlets. If these storehouses were suddenly depleted for any length of time, what would we expect to happen in our cities?

ORGANIZING A PLAN

Please remember that food storage is not an overnight project. It is a long-term goal operated successfully on a rotation basis.

1. Store only what your family eats and enjoys.

2. List the amount each member consumes on a daily basis and compute to weekly, monthly, and then work toward a goal of one year's supply.

3. Every time you need an item on your shopping list, purchase two or three items extra. This will build up your food supply. Be sure to watch for sales and use your store coupons.

4. Locate a cool, dark, well-insulated place for your food storage. Avoid areas with moisture and extreme heat, such as near refrigerators, dishwashers, water heaters, pipes, dryers, attics, laundry rooms, etc.

5. Areas of extreme temperatures can cause rapid deterioration of foods and cans to explode. Best temperature is between forty and fifty degrees Fahrenheit.

6. An ideal storage space is the basement. Do not store your food products directly on the concrete. Use wooden slats as shelving; otherwise, moisture can cause rusting and sweating of your canned foods.

7. Purchase dehydrated or freeze-dried foods in abundance, if possible, for these store for much longer periods.

8. Buy items in bulk whenever possible and always look for sales. You might consider purchasing the store brands; they offer considerable savings over the popular nationally advertised brands.

9. Consider making your own mixes and learn to save even more money.

WHAT TO STORE

This is a general list. After reading over the list, think of other items you may want to add.

Basic sewing supplies (scissors, needles, thread, etc.)

Battery-operated lanterns with batteries

Candles

Clothing materials (heavy and lightweight)

Diapers and other baby items

Disinfectants (liquid and spray)

Emergency first-aid kit

Flashlight with batteries

Fuel for cooking

Games, cards, etc. for family entertainment

Garbage bags and tall kitchen plastic bags

Heavy gloves

Lanterns with lamp oil

Large tub for washing clothes

Laundry detergent

Matches (keep in a waterproof jar)

Medical supplies and medicines

Outdoor cooking utensils (cast iron pots)

Paper products (cups, plates, utensils)

Paper, pens, and pencils

Quilts and blankets, bedding supplies

Soap without deodorants or colorings (unwrap for longer shelf life)

Toilet tissue and other sanitary products

Tools (hammer, nails, ax, saw, shovel, pliers, knives, rope)

Vegetable seeds for planting

USING YOUR FOOD STORAGE

With a felt-tip marker, date each product purchased or home canned, and place the perishable foods in a location of easy accessibility. The other items can be placed on your pantry shelves in a standard organized manner.

To master the plan of food rotation effectively, compile a list of foods eaten on a per-month basis. Remove the oldest cans on your list first from your pantry and place them on the kitchen cabinet shelf. (You are no longer keeping these foods in your storage room.) Use these items first, and replace the products from the list with newly purchased and dated ones. Use the oldest products first. This way you will have a working "rotated" food-storage program.

Check your food pantry periodically to notice whether your family's appetite changes. If a certain food accumulates in storage, you know it's time to reduce the supply of that item and replace it with other foods your family now prefers.

ABBREVIATIONS

STANDARD			METRIC		
tsp.	=	teaspoon	ml.	=	milliliter
tbsp.	=	tablespoon	l.	=	liter
oz.	=	ounce	g.	=	gram
qt.	=	quart	kg.	=	kilogram
lb.	=	pound	mg.	=	milligram

STANDARD-METRIC APPROXIMATIONS

⅛ teaspoon	=		.6 milliliter		
¼ teaspoon	=		1.2 milliliters		
½ teaspoon	=		2.5 milliliters		
1 teaspoon	=		5 milliliters		
1 tablespoon	=		15 milliliters		
4 tablespoons	=	¼ cup	=	60 milliliters	
8 tablespoons	=	½ cup	=	118 milliliters	
16 tablespoons	=	1 cup	=	236 milliliters	
2 cups	=		473 milliliters		
2½ cups	=		563 milliliters		
4 cups	=		946 milliliters		
1 quart	=	4 cups	=	.94 liter	

SOLID MEASUREMENTS

½ ounce	=		15 grams		
1 ounce	=		25 grams		
4 ounces	=		110 grams		
16 ounces	=	1 pound	=	454 grams	

CEREALS

BASIC COLD CEREAL MIX
An all-natural cereal packed with homemade freshness.

3 cups milk
2 tbsp. honey
1 tsp. vanilla extract
1 tsp. salt
1 cup brown sugar
2 cups whole-wheat flour or all-purpose flour
2 cups oatmeal, uncooked

Beat milk, honey, vanilla extract, and salt until well blended. In a separate bowl, combine dry ingredients. Pour milk mixture into dry ingredients and mix until smooth. Spread ¼" thick on 2 or 3 greased cookie sheets. Bake at 350 degrees for about 35 to 45 minutes or until golden crisp. Cool and break into flakes. Keep in a cool, dry place.
YIELDS: about 6 cups

GRANOLA CEREAL
There is nothing artificial here, just homemade goodness in every bowl.

4 cups quick oats, uncooked
1 cup coconut flakes
1 cup wheat germ
1 cup sunflower seeds, hulled
½ cup raisins
¾ cup chopped almonds
¾ cup honey
1 cup vegetable oil
1 tsp. vanilla extract

In a large mixing bowl, combine all dry ingredients. In a saucepan heat honey, oil, and vanilla extract until thin and well blended. Pour liquid over dry ingredients. Stir until well coated. Spread mixture thinly in a shallow pan. Place in a 300-degree oven for about 20 minutes, stirring every 5 minutes until lightly browned. Store in an airtight container and keep in a cool, dry place.

YIELDS: about 8 cups

INSTANT OATMEAL

Makes a quick breakfast in less than two minutes. This oatmeal is delicious with fresh fruit, honey, cinnamon sugar, or cream and butter.

½ cup quick oats
⅛ tsp. salt

Combine oats and salt. Store in 3"x5" clear zip-type bags. These inexpensive bags can be purchased at Wal-Mart and craft stores. For instant oatmeal, empty oatmeal packet into a microwave bowl. Add 1¼ cups water. Stir. Microwave on high for about 1½ minutes. **Caution:** Bowl will be very hot.

YIELDS: 1 serving

POWER-UP BREAKFAST BARS

Just the right snack to keep you energized.

½ cup honey
½ cup creamy peanut butter
2½ cups Granola Cereal (see recipe)
½ cup raisins
½ cup nonfat powdered dry milk

Blend honey with peanut butter. Add remaining ingredients and continue to blend well. Mold into bars or cookies. Wrap in plastic. Refrigerate.

YIELDS: about 24 small bars

Almost Pop Tarts

Don't settle for the boxed kind. Make it your way and save.

1 can refrigerated pie dough
Jam (flavor of your choice)

Take pie dough, roll out as usual, and cut into rectangles. Spread jam on half of them, leaving ½" or so border without jam. Cover with the other half of the rectangle. Crimp edges with a fork to seal. Bake until the pie dough is done. Frost when completely cooled, if desired.

Yields: about 12 tarts

Frosting Mix for Tarts

1 cup confectioners' sugar
¼ tsp. vanilla extract
2 tsp. water

In a small bowl, combine confections' sugar and vanilla extract. Gradually add water in small amounts while stirring to obtain the right consistency. Blend to a smooth and creamy texture. Add less or more water to make spreadable.

Yields: about ½ cup

RAISIN AND BRAN CEREAL
An all-natural cereal with a country-time flavor.

¼ cup vegetable oil
1 tbsp. honey or molasses
1 cup water
2 cups bran
2 cups wheat flour
1 tsp. salt
1 cup raisins

Beat oil, honey, and water until well blended. In a separate bowl, combine all dry ingredients, except raisins. Make a well in center and add liquid mixture. Thoroughly mix together. Divide into 3 parts. Roll each part to very thin, no more than ⅛" thick, and spread on greased cookie sheet. Bake in a 350-degree oven for about 15 to 20 minutes or until lightly browned and crisp. If not completely dry, turn oven off and let set longer. Break into flakes and add raisins. Store in an airtight container in a cool, dry place. YIELDS: about 1 lb.

WHEAT FLAKES CEREAL

Homemade cereal the way you like. Top it with fresh fruits.

1½ cups whole-wheat flour
¼ cup all-purpose flour
¼ cup wheat germ
¾ tsp. salt
¼ cup creamy peanut butter
¾ cup water

Blend flours, wheat germ, and salt together. In a separate bowl, beat peanut butter with water until mixture is smooth. Add dry ingredients and knead into a soft workable dough. Add additional water if needed. Roll out, no more than ⅛" thick, on a lightly floured board and place onto a greased cookie sheet. Bake in a 350-degree oven for about 15 minutes or until lightly browned. Break into small pieces and store in an airtight container.

YIELDS: about 10 oz.

PANCAKES, WAFFLES, AND MUFFINS

BLUEBERRY SYRUP

Enjoy this recipe even more by using freshly picked raspberries or blackberries.

2 cups fresh blueberries
1 cup sugar
1 cup brown sugar
1 cup cornstarch
1 tsp. vanilla extract

Crush blueberries with a potato masher. Reserve juice and add just enough water to equal 1 cup. Combine liquid and all ingredients with mashed blueberries in a large saucepan. Bring mixture to a boil and cook gently for about 3 minutes, stirring continuously. Be careful not to burn mixture. When cooled, store in a tightly sealed jar and keep refrigerated.
YIELDS: about 2 cups

MAPLE SYRUP

1 cup sugar
1 cup light brown sugar
1 cup corn syrup
1cup water
1½ tsp. maple extract

Combine all ingredients, except maple extract, in a saucepan and bring to a boil. Reduce heat. Cook gently, stirring constantly until thickened. This takes about 4 minutes. Stir in maple extract. When cooled, store in a tightly sealed jar and keep refrigerated.
YIELDS: about 2 cups

Basic Pancake Mix

4 cups all-purpose flour
4 tbsp. sugar
4 tsp. baking powder

Sift all ingredients together. Store in an airtight container in a cool, dry place. Use when making homemade pancakes (see recipe).
Yields: 4 cups

Pancakes

1 cup Basic Pancake Mix (see recipe)
1 egg, beaten
¾ cup milk

Blend all ingredients, making sure not to overmix. Do not beat. Fry in lightly oiled pan until browned on both sides.
Yields: 3 pancakes

Basic Buckwheat Pancake Mix

1 cup buckwheat flour
1 cup whole-wheat flour
2 tsp. baking powder
1 tsp. baking soda
2 tsp. sugar
1 tsp. salt

Sift all ingredients together twice. Store in an airtight container in a cool, dry place.
Yields: 2 cups

BUCKWHEAT PANCAKES
The buttermilk adds an exceptionally rich taste to this mix.

1 cup Basic Buckwheat Pancake Mix (see recipe)
1 egg, separated
2 tbsp. butter, melted
1 cup buttermilk

Mix Buckwheat Pancake Mix, egg yolk, butter, and buttermilk together in a bowl. Beat egg white until stiff. Fold into batter. Stir to blend. Cook on lightly greased skillet until browned on both sides. Serve with butter and maple syrup.
YIELDS: 3 pancakes

WAFFLES

2 cups all-purpose flour
2 tsp. baking powder
⅓ tsp. salt
3 eggs, separated
½ tsp. vanilla extract
1⅔ cups milk
¼ cup butter, melted

Sift first 3 ingredients together. Thoroughly beat egg yolks and vanilla. Blend with milk and butter. Add flour mixture and mix until well blended. Let batter rest about 1 hour in refrigerator. With electric mixer, beat egg whites until stiff and fold into the batter. Oil waffle iron and fill ⅔ full of the batter. Cook until done.
YIELDS: 4 waffles

ENGLISH MUFFINS

This scrumptious muffin complements any spread.

1 package yeast
1 cup warm water
1 cup warm milk
2 tbsp. sugar
1 tsp. salt
3 tbsp. butter, melted
5 to 6 cups all-purpose flour
Cornmeal

In a mixing bowl, dissolve yeast in warm water. Let set 2 minutes. Blend in milk, sugar, salt, and butter. Add 3 cups flour and beat until smooth. Gradually work in enough remaining flour to knead dough until smooth and elastic. Place in a greased bowl. Turn over once. Let rise until doubled in size. Punch down and divide dough into 2 parts. Sprinkle board with cornmeal and roll into ½" thickness. Cut into circles to desired size. Place on greased cookie sheets in a warm place to rise until doubled. Fry on a lightly oiled skillet with cornmeal side down. Cook until lightly browned on each side. Split muffins in half and serve. Toast, later, if desired.

YIELDS: about 18 small muffins

BLUEBERRY MUFFIN BASIC MIX

These plan-ahead packages are made to save you time and money.

2½ tsp. baking powder
1¾ cups all-purpose flour
2 tbsp. sugar
¾ tsp. salt

Sift all ingredients together. Package in a zip-type bag and store in a cool, dry place. Use in Blueberry Muffin recipe.
YIELDS: 1 packet

BLUEBERRY MUFFINS

These are so delectable you'll think they were made at a bakery.

¾ cup blueberries, fresh or frozen
1 packet Blueberry Muffin Basic Mix (see recipe)
1 egg, beaten
½ cup milk
⅓ cup melted butter

If blueberries are frozen, thaw and pat dry. Combine all ingredients in a bowl. Stir only until dry ingredients are moistened. Spoon batter into paper muffin cups. Bake in a 400-degree oven for about 25 minutes or until done.
YIELDS: about 12 muffins

SNACKS

FROZEN FUDGE POPS

3 tbsp. all-purpose flour
1 cup sugar
4 cups milk
3½ tbsp. cocoa
Popsicle sticks

Combine all ingredients in a saucepan and stir over medium heat. Boil for 1 minute, making sure mixture is thoroughly blended. Pour into Styrofoam cups and freeze. Add sticks to cups when mixture is cold enough to hold them straight up.
YIELDS: 12 pops

PUDDING ON A STICK

1 package instant pudding
Paper cups
Popsicle sticks

Follow directions on packaged instant pudding mix. Pour into 3-oz. paper cups. Cover tops with aluminum foil. Insert sticks in center of each cup. Put in freezer. When frozen, peel off the paper cup and enjoy.
YIELDS: 8 servings

HEALTHY APPLE POPS

4 cups apple juice
1 cup applesauce
Popsicle sticks

In a bowl, combine juice and applesauce. Stir to blend. Pour into ice cube trays and freeze. When almost frozen, insert sticks.
YIELDS: 18 pops

FRUIT COCKTAIL

This unique combination of juices adds a delightful flavor to this cool fruit snack.

1 cup diced peaches with juice
1 small jar cherries with juice, cut in halves
1 cup pineapple chunks with juice
1 cup diced pears with juice
½ cup orange juice
2 tbsp. lemon juice concentrate

In a large bowl, mix all ingredients together and chill. Keep refrigerated in a closed container.
YIELDS: about 38 oz.

CARAMEL CORN

2 qt. popped popcorn
½ cup peanuts, shelled and skinless
¼ cup light brown sugar
3 tbsp. margarine
¼ cup light corn syrup
¼ cup light molasses
½ tsp. salt
¼ tsp. baking soda
¾ tsp. vanilla extract

Place popcorn and peanuts in a deep buttered pan. Combine sugar, margarine, corn syrup, molasses, and salt in saucepan and heat until boiling. Boil without stirring until temperature reaches 250 degrees F on a candy thermometer. Remove from heat immediately and add the baking soda and vanilla. Stir until well blended. Pour mixture over popcorn and peanuts and mix well with spatula. Spread caramel corn into a shallow pan and bake in a 250-degree oven for about 1 hour, stirring occasionally. Let cool. With spatula, lift caramel corn from pan and break into bite-size pieces. Store in an airtight container in a cool, dry place.
YIELDS: about 8 cups

ITALIAN-FLAVORED POPCORN

This delicious gourmet popcorn will draw everyone's attention to your creativeness. Better make an extra batch.

2 qt. popped popcorn, kept warm
½ cup butter or margarine, melted
Shaker container of Kraft Grated Three-Cheese Blend

Spread warm popcorn on a cookie sheet. Drizzle with melted butter or margarine followed by a generous sprinkling of cheese. Serve hot.
YIELDS: 2 qt.

CREOLE PRALINES

1½ cups milk
3 cups sugar
1 tsp. vanilla extract
1 cup shelled pecans, chopped

Cook milk and sugar until soft-ball stage (235 to 240 degrees F) on a candy thermometer. Add vanilla extract and pecans. Cook to 240 degrees F. Pour small patties onto buttered cookie sheets or plates and allow to cool. They will harden when cooled. When completely cool, wrap individually in waxed paper.
YIELDS: about 2 dozen pralines

PEANUT BUTTER CUPS

These are so delicious and make a perfect party favorite. Have your own candy factory right at home.

1 24-oz. chocolate-flavored almond bar
1 package mini baking cups
1 18-oz. container creamy peanut butter

In a glass bowl, heat the almond bar on high for about 1½ minutes in microwave or use double boiler until melted. Fill bottom of muffin cups with ½ tsp. of melted chocolate. Add ½ tsp. peanut butter to each one and fill the tops with remaining melted chocolate. Let set in a cool place until firm to the touch. (**Hint:** Adding powdered confectioners' sugar to peanut butter and rolling into small-size marbles will make it less messy when placing the peanut butter inside the paper cups using the teaspoon method.) Use as much confectioners' sugar as you need to make molding easier.

YIELDS: about 30 peanut butter cups

PEANUT BRITTLE

2 cups sugar
1 cup light corn syrup
1 cup water
2 cups peanuts, unsalted and skinless
¼ tsp. salt
1 tsp. butter
¼ tsp. baking soda

Combine sugar, corn syrup, and water in a large pot. Cook over medium heat, stirring constantly until sugar dissolves. Cook slowly, without stirring, until the syrup reaches soft-ball stage on a candy thermometer. (At this point, syrup dropped into a glass of cold water will form a pliable ball.) Add the peanuts and salt to the syrup and stir. Cook to the hard-crack stage (300 to 310 degrees F) on the candy thermometer, stirring constantly. Add butter and baking soda. Stir to blend. Pour as patties onto large buttered plates or buttered cookie sheets. Brittle will harden when cooled. Crack into desired sizes. Store in an airtight container in a cool, dry place.

YIELDS: about 3 lb.

PEANUT CLUSTERS

2 small bags chocolate chips
1 small bag butterscotch chips
2 16-oz. jars salted peanuts

Melt chocolate and butterscotch chips on low heat or use microwave. Stir constantly to keep from burning. Mix peanuts with melted chocolate and butterscotch. Remove from heat. Place by teaspoonfuls on greased cookie sheets or parchment paper. The clusters will harden when cooled.
YIELDS: about 3½ lb.

BASIC GRANOLA MIX

4 cups quick oats, uncooked
1 cup coconut flakes
¾ cup wheat germ
¾ cup almonds, chopped
⅔ cup brown sugar
½ cup nonfat dry milk (optional)

Combine all ingredients together. Store in an airtight container in a cool, dry place. Use in Granola Bar recipe.
YIELDS: about 7 cups

Granola Bars

½ cup honey
½ tsp. almond or vanilla extract
½ tsp. salt
12 tbsp. butter, melted
½ cup brown sugar
5½ cups Basic Granola Mix (see recipe)

In a large mixing bowl, thoroughly blend honey, extract, salt, and butter. Add sugar and granola mix. Mix until well blended. Press into greased shallow, rectangle pan. Bake in a 350-degree oven for about 15 to 20 minutes or until lightly browned and bubbly. Cut into bars and wrap individually. Store in a cool, dry place.
Yields: 12 bars

Trail Mix

3 cups roasted, salted peanuts
1 cup salted sunflower seeds
¾ cup raisins
½ cup M&M's
¾ cup coconut flakes
1 cup chocolate chips
1 cup dried banana chips
1½ cups pretzel sticks
Figs and dates, chopped (optional)

Combine all ingredients into a large zip-type plastic bag. Shake to blend well. Store in a cool, dry place in a glass jar with a tight-fitting lid.
Yields: 9 cups

Raisin Almond Crunch

2 qt. popped popcorn
1 cup raisins
1 cup toasted slivered almonds
1 cup coconut flakes
½ cup butter
¾ cup light corn syrup
½ tsp. almond extract

Combine first four ingredients together in a bowl. In a 4-qt. saucepan, heat butter and corn syrup to boiling, stirring occasionally. Remove from heat and stir in almond extract. Add popcorn mixture and toss to coat evenly. Spread in a shallow pan and bake in a 350-degree oven for about 15 minutes, stirring often. Loosen from pan and cool. Store in an airtight container in a cool, dry place.
Yields: about 5 cups

Hard Candy

3¾ cups sugar
1½ cups light corn syrup
1 cup water
1 tsp. oil flavoring (peppermint, etc.)
Food coloring (optional)

In a large saucepan, mix sugar, corn syrup, and water. Stir the mixture over medium heat until all the sugar is dissolved. Let boil, without stirring, until temperature reaches 310 degrees F or until drops of syrup form hard, brittle threads in cold water. Remove from heat. When boiling has stopped, stir in the flavoring. Add food coloring, if desired. Pour into a lightly greased cookie sheet. Let cool then break into pieces.
Yields: at least 15 bite-sized pieces

Almost-Heavenly Hash

1 lb. solid milk chocolate
12 marshmallows, chopped fine
¾ cups chopped almonds

Melt chocolate in a double boiler or microwave. Line a tray with parchment paper. Pour half the melted chocolate in the tray and cover with the chopped marshmallows and nuts. Cover mixture with remaining chocolate. Let cool thoroughly before cutting into pieces.
Yields: 8 pieces

Heavenly Fudge

4½ cups sugar
1 12-oz. can evaporated milk
8 oz. miniature marshmallows
18 oz. chocolate chips
½ cup butter
2 cups chopped nuts
1 tsp. vanilla extract

In a large pot, combine sugar and milk. Bring to a strong rolling boil, sitrring constantly. Boil hard for about 5 to 8 minutes. Be careful. This mixture will be very hot. Keep stirring to prevent burning. Remove from heat. Add marshmallows, chocolate, and butter. Stir until melted and blended well. Add nuts and extract. Mix all ingredients together. Spread on ungreased pan. Let cool. Cut into squares.
Yields: about 8 pieces

Ice Cream in a Bag

This is an amazing recipe for homemade ice cream in just 5 minutes. Try other flavored extracts for a different taste.

1 gallon-size, zip-type plastic bag
Ice cubes
6 tbsp. rock salt (called Ice Cream Salt)
½ cup milk
¼ tsp. vanilla extract
1 tbsp. sugar
1 pint-size, zip-type plastic bag

Fill the gallon-size bag half full of ice cubes. Add the rock salt and seal the bag tight. Pour the milk, vanilla, and sugar into the small bag and seal it. Place the small bag inside the large bag and seal again carefully. Shake until mixture becomes ice cream (about 5 minutes). Remove the small sealed bag with ice cream from the larger bag. Discard the large bag. Wipe off the top of the small bag and open carefully to empty out the ice cream. Add crushed cookies and chocolate chips to this ice cream for a super snack.
YIELDS: 1 serving

ICE CREAM SANDWICHES

Use your favorite ice cream to fill these sandwiches.

1 egg, beaten
½ cup solid vegetable shortening
¼ cup butter, softened to room temperature
1 tsp. vanilla extract
1 box Devil's Food Cake mix
Ice cream

In a mixing bowl, cream together egg, shortening, butter, and vanilla. Add half box of cake mix and continue to mix until blended well. Add remaining cake mix and work into a smooth dough. Roll dough onto a lightly floured board to about ¼" thickness. Cut into pairs of squares or large rounds of equal sizes and place on greased cookie pans. Bake 8 to 10 minutes at 375 degrees. When fresh from the oven, poke holes, with a fork, into the cakes. Let cool completely before spreading ice cream between layers. Wrap individually in wax paper. Keep frozen until ready to eat.
YIELDS: 8 sandwiches

POTATO CHIPS

You can make these delicious all-natural potato chips cheaply. Try this with your food processor.

First, attach the thin slicing blade. Choose small whole potatoes and peel off the skins. Process. Place quickly in a bowl of water to remove the excess starch. Go through the batch discarding the tiny pieces. Keep chips in water until ready to fry. Drain in a colander and pat lightly with towel only the amount needed for your next batch. Start with fresh oil and reserve this same oil after straining for other batches of potato chips. Potatoes pick up the taste of other foods very easily when fried in used oil. When your chips reach a golden brown color and appear crisp, about 5 minutes, drain into a wire basket, shaking the basket several times over hot oil. Dump into a platter lined with paper towels. This will help absorb the excess oil and take away the extra greasiness. Salt lightly. Enjoy experimenting with other seasoning powders such as barbeque and garlic instead of plain salt.

TORTILLA CHIPS

Enjoy these freshly baked chips dusted with your favorite finely ground seasonings.

3 cups all-purpose flour
1 cup yellow cornmeal
4 tsp. baking powder
1 tbsp. solid vegetable shortening
1 egg, beaten
1 cup water
Oil for frying
Popcorn Salt (see recipe)

In a mixing bowl, sift together the flour, cornmeal, and baking powder. Cut in shortening with pastry blender until mixture feels crumbly. Add beaten egg and water and form into a stiff pliable dough. Knead, by hand, for 6 minutes or use a food processor. Divide dough into 4 parts. Roll out each part into 10" squares ⅛" thick. Cut again into 2" squares. Divide each of the squares into 2 triangles. Fry in hot oil for about 2 minutes or until golden brown on both sides. Drain on paper towels. Sprinkle with Popcorn Salt. Cool. Store in an airtight container.
YIELDS: about 1 lb.

SALTS, SEASONINGS, AND SPICES

No-Salt Salt

A simple mixture packed with lots of flavor.

5 tsp. onion powder
1 tbsp. garlic powder
1 tbsp. dry mustard
1 tbsp. paprika
1 tsp. powdered thyme
½ tsp. white pepper
½ tsp. finely ground celery seed (optional)

Mix all ingredients together and pour into an airtight shaker container. Store in a cool, dry place. Use instead of salt.
Yields: about ¼ cup

Salt Substitute

A quickly made recipe using simple ingredients most people have on their pantry shelves.

4 tsp. onion powder
4 tsp. garlic powder
2 tsp. paprika
1 tsp. white pepper

Mix all ingredients and pour into an airtight salt shaker. Use in place of salt.
Yields: about ¼ cup

SEASONED SALT SUBSTITUTE

Bring out the flavor of salads with a few shakes of this mix. In your salad, use apple or lemon juice in place of vinegar and oil for an unusal experience.

1 tsp. sage
1 tsp. basil
1 tsp. marjoram
1 tsp. ground thyme
1 tsp. parsley flakes
1 tsp. savory (optional)
1 tsp. mace (optional)
1 tsp. onion powder
1 tsp. garlic powder
¼ tsp. cayenne pepper or chili powder
¼ tsp. black pepper

Mix all ingredients and process in a blender until powdery. Store in an airtight container in a cool, dry place. Use in place of salt.
YIELDS: about ¼ cup

POPCORN SALT

This is one of those little-known secrets food wholesalers hoped you'd never find out.

¼ cup table salt

Pour salt in an electric blender and blend on highest speed for about 20 seconds or until powdery. Store in an airtight container in a cool, dry place. Try this salt on french fries. **Note:** Popcorn salt is just simply a very fine-grained salt that sticks much better on popcorn than regular table salt. Start counting your savings now.
YIELDS: about ¼ cup

CAJUN SEASONING

For spicy Southern flavor, use this to season chicken.

13 oz. plain salt
3 tbsp. lemon pepper
1 tsp. finely ground, dry red pepper
1 tbsp. garlic powder
1 tbsp. chili powder
1 tsp. ground thyme
1 tsp. filé powder
1 tsp. finely ground basil

Mix all ingredients and store in an airtight container in a cool, dry place. Use in place of salt.
YIELDS: about 14 oz.

CREOLE SEASONING

Bring the taste of Louisiana right into your kitchen with this favorite old-time recipe.

1½ cups salt
3 tbsp. lemon pepper
1 tbsp. chili powder
1½ tbsp. garlic powder
1½ tsp. onion powder
⅛ tsp. celery salt
1½ tbsp finely ground, dry red pepper
Ground ginger, to taste

Mix all ingredients and store in an airtight container in a cool, dry place. Use in place of salt.
YIELDS: about 1¾ cups

SEAFOOD SEASONING

Excellent on fish, shrimp, crab cakes, and other seafood dishes.

1 cup salt
1 tbsp. black pepper
1 tsp. chili powder
1 tbsp. garlic powder
½ tsp. thyme
½ tsp. dry, ground basil
⅛ tsp. celery salt
3 tbsp. lemon pepper
1 tbsp. ground, dry red pepper
Dash of ground ginger

   Combine all ingredients and store in an airtight container in a cool, dry place. Use instead of salt.
YIELDS: about 1¼ cups

PLAIN FISH FRY MIX

This good basic mix has not been spiced up.

¾ cup all-purpose flour
2 tbsp. cornstarch
¼ tsp. baking soda
¼ tsp. baking powder
¼ tsp. salt

   Combine all ingredients and store in an airtight zip-top bag in a cool, dry place. Label.
YIELDS: 1 packet

CREOLE SEAFOOD FISH FRY MIX

The lemon pepper seasoning in this mix will freshen up your next fish fry.

4 tbsp. parsley flakes
2 tbsp. lemon pepper
2 tbsp. celery seed
2 tbsp. ground, dry thyme
2 tbsp. marjoram
2 tsp. onion powder
2 bay leaves, finely ground
2 tsp. garlic powder

Combine all ingredients together in a large bowl. Store in an airtight jar in a cool, dry place. Label.
YIELDS: about ¾ cup

CRAB BOIL

An easy-to-make recipe that can be stored in quart-size, zip-type bags for later use.

2 cups salt
2 tbsp. black pepper
2 tsp. celery seeds
2 tbsp. cayenne pepper
8 bay leaves, crushed
½ tsp. ground thyme
2 tbsp. dried parsley
½ tsp. cloves
1 tsp. ground ginger
½ tsp. allspice

Thoroughly mix all ingredients. Divide into 2 packets. Store in an airtight container in a cool, dry place. To use: Add 1 packet of Crab Boil to 1 gallon of boiling water. Boil crabs until done.
YIELDS: 2 packets (1¼ cups per packet)

SHRIMP BOIL

You'll want to double this recipe if you have more shrimp. Add small red potatoes to the boiling water and your neighbors will want to join the festivities.

½ cup salt
½ tsp. cloves
½ tsp. allspice
½ tsp. black pepper
¼ tsp. cayenne pepper
1 tbsp. dehydrated minced garlic
2 tbsp. dried minced onions
2 tbsp. dried celery flakes
5 bay leaves, crushed
1 tbsp. dried parsley
½ tsp. red pepper flakes

Combine all ingredients and mix well. Store in a glass jar with a tight-fitting lid. To use: For boiling 2 to 3 lb. of shrimp, use 5 tbsp. Shrimp Boil to a ½ gallon of salted water. Cook shrimp until done.
YIELDS: ¾ cup

ITALIAN SEASONING

Never run out of Italian seasoning again! Delicious as a dipping sauce for bread when gently blended with olive oil.

2 tbsp. dried basil
2 tbsp. dried marjoram
2 tbsp. oregano
1½ tsp. ground sage

Combine all ingredients and store in an airtight container in a cool, dry place.
YIELDS: ¼ cup

POULTRY SEASONING

Season up your chicken or hen with this excellent blend of herbs and spices. Excellent when used in homemade stuffing.

2 tbsp. lemon pepper or black pepper
1 tsp. nutmeg
4 tbsp. dried parsley, crushed
4 tbsp. ground sage
4 tbsp. ground thyme
2 tbsp. ground marjoram
2 tbsp. ground rosemary
2 tbsp. savory

Blend all ingredients and store in an airtight container in a cool, dry place.
YIELDS: 1¼ cups

CURRY POWDER

Experience the flavor of Indian culture. Add to taste in your favorite soups and stews.

2 tbsp. coriander seeds
2 tbsp. cumin seeds
2 tbsp. cardamom seeds
1 tsp. dry mustard seeds
1 tsp. cayenne pepper
1 tsp. turmeric

Toast coriander, cumin, and cardamom seeds in a 200-degree oven for about 20 minutes, stirring occasionally. Let cool. Grind the toasted seeds and all remaining ingredients together. This powder is best when used within 6 months.
YIELDS: about ½ cup

TENNESSEE DRY RUB

The perfect blend of seasonings to bring out the best of beef, chicken, or pork.

⅔ cups brown sugar
2 tbsp. white pepper
2 tbsp. paprika
½ tsp. chili powder or cayenne pepper
1½ tbsp. salt
2 tsp. onion powder
1 tbsp. garlic powder

Mix all ingredients and store in an airtight container in a cool, dry place. To use: Simply rub meats on all sides with the mixture and cook in the oven to penetrate the flavor into the meats. (I would not suggest you cook the meats directly on the grill.)

COAT-AND-COOK MIX

This seasoning mix is perfect for coating chicken or pork for baking in the oven.

1 cup all-purpose flour
1 tsp. black pepper
½ cup grated saltine crackers
1 tsp. thyme
1 tsp. dried sweet basil
1 tbsp. Italian Seasoning (see recipe)
1 tsp. dried sage
1 tsp. paprika
¼ tsp. nutmeg (optional)
½ tsp. garlic powder
½ tsp. onion powder

Mix all ingredients together until well blended. Store in an airtight container in a cool, dry place. This recipe can be made in bulk by doubling the measurements.

YIELDS: about 1¾ cups

SAUCES

CRANBERRY SAUCE (JELLIED)

You cannot find a fresher cranberry sauce than this one! It's great for the holidays.

4¼ cups fresh cranberries
1¾ cups water
2 cups sugar

Prepare berries by washing, sorting, and stemming them. In a large pot, boil berries and water together until skins burst. Press through a sieve. Add sugar to the pulp and the juice. Mix well. Boil almost to gelling point on candy thermometer, 220 F (sea level to 1000 feet), or when jelly breaks from the spoon in a sheet or flake. Ladle hot sauce into sterilized, hot Ball-type canning jars, leaving ¼" headspace. Wipe the top rims of the jars and adjust caps and lids. Place in a boiling water canner, covering the tops of jars with 1" of water. Process 10 minutes in canner.
YIELDS: about 2 pt.

CRANBERRY SAUCE (WHOLE)

Using this same recipe, you can substitute similar berries for cranberries.

8 cups fresh cranberries
4 cups sugar
4 cups water

Prepare cranberries by washing, sorting, and stemming them. In a large saucepot, boil sugar and water for 5 minutes. Add cranberries. Continue boiling without stirring until skins burst. Ladle hot sauce into hot, sterilized Ball-type canning jars, leaving ¼" headspace. Wipe the top rims of the jars and adjust caps and lids. Place in a boiling water canner, covering the tops of jars with 1" of water. Process 10 minutes in canner.
YIELDS: about 6 pt.

BARBEQUE SAUCE
Add this delicious sauce to your pork and beans.

2 15-oz. cans tomato sauce
½ cup vegetable oil
½ cup brown sugar
1 tsp. ground allspice
½ cup water
¼ cup Worcestershire sauce
1 tsp. black pepper
1 tbsp. hot sauce
1 tsp. celery seed
⅛ tsp. horseradish
Juice of 1 lemon
¾ tsp. garlic powder
¾ tsp. onion powder
2 tbsp. vinegar
1 tbsp. liquid smoke (optional)
1 tsp. dry mustard

In a 2-qt. saucepan, combine all ingredients. Heat to bubbly, stirring constantly to keep from sticking. Immediately reduce heat and simmer for 15 to 20 minutes.
YIELDS: 46 oz.

Basic Mix for Chili Sauce

This mix makes a chili so good you will want to use it on hamburgers, too.

2 tsp. onion powder
2 tsp. garlic powder
5 tsp. chili powder
1 tbsp. all-purpose flour
1 tsp. salt
½ tsp. ground cumin
½ tsp. sugar

Blend all ingredients together and store in a zip-type bag in a cool place.
YIELDS: 1 packet

Curry Sauce

Flavors will be enhanced if this sauce is made a day before serving.

1 cup mayonnaise
½ tbsp. Curry Powder (see recipe)
½ tbsp. ketchup
½ tbsp. chopped chutney
¼ tsp. applesauce

Blend mayonnaise and curry together. Add ketchup, chutney, and applesauce and mix thoroughly. Store in a tightly closed container in the refrigerator.
YIELDS: about 1 cup

HOLLANDAISE SAUCE

You'll love this sauce over your favorite broiled salmon dish.

2 tbsp. lemon juice
4 egg yolks, beaten
2 sticks butter, melted
Dash of salt

Stir lemon juice into beaten egg yolks and blend well. Cook over double boiler on low heat. Gradually add melted butter and salt to taste. Stir constantly until mixture appears thickened. Store in the refrigerator.
YIELDS: about 1 cup

HONEY MUSTARD SAUCE

This is absolutely the best you've ever tasted!

¼ cup mayonnaise
¼ cup prepared mustard
2 tbsp. honey
1 tsp. brown sugar

Cream all ingredients together until smooth. Store in a jar or squeeze bottle. Keep refrigerated.
YIELDS: 4 oz.

HORSERADISH SAUCE

The perfect condiment for hamburgers and hot dogs.

1 cup mayonnaise
½ cup sour cream
¾ tbsp. horseradish
Dash of white pepper

Combine all ingredients together until well blended. Store in a closed jar in the refrigerator.

YIELDS: about 1½ cups

TARTAR SAUCE

Homemade tartar sauce is the perfect match for your favorite seafood.

½ cup mayonnaise
2 tbsp. dill pickle, finely chopped
2 tbsp. green onion, finely chopped
1 tsp. grated lemon peel
2 tsp. lemon juice

Mix all ingredients together until well blended. Store in an airtight container in the refrigerator.

YIELDS: ½ cup

Sweet and Sour Sauce

This delicious sauce is great served with ham.

1 cup brown sugar
2 tbsp. cornstarch
¼ tsp. salt
¼ tsp. ground cinnamon
Dash of ground cloves
6 oz. pineapple juice
½ cup vinegar
¼ cup lemon juice

Combine sugar, cornstarch, salt, and spices in a saucepan. Stir until well blended. Gradually add pineapple juice, vinegar, and lemon juice. Cook over medium-low heat, stirring constantly until thickened.

Yields: about 1¾ cups

Teriyaki Sauce

Bet you didn't think you could make your own teriyaki sauce. Here is the secret.

½ cup soy sauce
⅓ cup water
2 thin slices of fresh ginger, minced
1 large clove garlic, minced
¼ cup sake or dry rice wine
2 tbsp. sugar

Combine soy sauce, water, ginger, and garlic in an electric blender. Mix on high speed until smooth. Pour mixture into a bowl and stir in sake and sugar. Store in an airtight container in the refrigerator.

Yields: about 1 cup

Pizza Sauce Mix

Making this mix will save you a lot of money over the brand-name packages. This says quality every time.

¼ cup grated Parmesan cheese
2 tsp. Italian seasoning
1 tsp. onion flakes
½ tsp. garlic powder
½ tsp. sugar

Mix all ingredients together and store in a zip-top bag (3"x5") found at Wal-Mart and craft shops. Use for making Pizza Sauce.
YIELDS: 1 packet

Pizza Sauce

1 packet Pizza Sauce Mix (see recipe)
1 15-oz. can tomato sauce

Combine mix with tomato sauce in a saucepan over medium heat, stirring occasionally. Cook for about 10 minutes.
YIELDS: 15 oz.

Spaghetti Sauce Seasoning Mix

This is a perfect blend of herbs and spices to create a sauce that is rich in both quality and taste.

2 tsp. grated Parmesan cheese
½ tsp. sugar
¼ tsp. onion powder
1 tsp. dried parsley flakes
¼ tsp. salt
¼ tsp. oregano powder
¼ tsp. basil powder
¼ tsp. garlic powder

Combine all ingredients together. Store in a clear, 2"x3" zip-top bag. Use for making Spaghetti Sauce.
Yields: 1 packet

Spaghetti Sauce

The taste says Italy! A delicious mild flavor spaghetti sauce that beats the name brands.

1 packet Spaghetti Sauce Seasoning Mix (see recipe)
¼ cup olive oil
2 6-oz. cans tomato paste
32 oz. water

In a large saucepan, combine 1 packet mix with olive oil. Cook on medium heat for a few minutes to "wake up the herbs and seasonings." Add tomato paste and water and stir continuously until spaghetti sauce is hot. Lower heat and cover, stirring often to keep sauce from sticking. The sauce is ready to serve over pasta in just 25 minutes. (The longer the simmering time the more flavorful the taste.) Refrigerate left over sauce. For a heartier sauce, add cooked Italian sausage or mushrooms.
Yields: 46 oz.

STROGANOFF SAUCE

This restaurant-quality sauce saves you and your family the expense of a night out.

1 clove garlic, finely chopped
½ cup minced onions
2 tbsp. butter
2 tbsp. all-purpose flour
¼ tsp. black pepper
1 4-oz. can mushrooms, sliced and drained (optional)
1 10¾-oz. can condensed cream of mushroom soup
1 cup sour cream
2 tbsp. ketchup (optional)
2 tbsp. minced fresh parsley

In a saucepan on medium heat, sauté garlic and onions in butter until tender. Gradually stir in flour, pepper, and mushrooms (optional) and sauté 1 minute longer. Stir in soup, sour cream, ketchup (optional), and parslely and blend well. Cook 10 minutes until sauce is hot. Serve over hot, cooked egg noodles. For a more filling meal, add cooked ground meat to sauce.
YIELDS: 30 oz.

ALFREDO SAUCE

It has to be all the rich cheeses, creams, and butter that make this a superb sauce.

8 oz. cream cheese, broken into small pieces
¾ cup grated Parmesan cheese
½ cup butter
¼ tsp. garlic powder
⅛ tsp. black pepper
1 cup milk or half-and-half

Combine all ingredients into a saucepan or skillet and heat on medium low. Stir continuously until mixture is thick and creamy, adding more milk if needed to obtain a desired consistency. Serve over hot, cooked fettuccine pasta.

YIELDS: about 2 cups

ALFREDO NOODLE SEASONING MIX

This mix is a lot cheaper than the store bought.

1 cup instant nonfat dry milk
2 tsp. grated Romano or Parmesan cheese
½ cup dried minced onion
1 tsp. garlic powder
½ tsp. salt
1 to 2 tsp. white pepper

Measure all ingredients into a closed airtight container. Shake to blend. Store in a cool, dry place. Use for making Alfredo Noodle Sauce.

YIELDS: 1½ cups

ALFREDO NOODLES SAUCE
This rich, one-pot sauce is so easy to make.

¼ cup Alfredo Noodle Seasoning Mix (see recipe)
2 tbsp. melted butter
¼ cup half-and-half

Combine all ingredients in a glass jar with a tight fitting lid. Shake to blend. Transfer to a saucepan and heat on medium, stirring constantly until well heated. Pour over hot, cooked noodles.
YIELDS: 4 oz.

BASIC WHITE SAUCE MIX
This basic mix can be adjusted to make a thin, medium, or thick white sauce and can be used as a thickener for soups and gravies. Experiment by adding chicken or beef bouillon (crushed) for a creamier soup or gravy.

2¾ cups nonfat dry milk
½ cup cornstarch
¼ tsp. white pepper

Sift all ingredients together. Keep in a tightly closed container in a cool, dry place. Mix again before each use.
YIELDS: 3¼ cups

THIN WHITE SAUCE

2 tbsp. butter
⅓ cup Basic White Sauce Mix (see recipe)
1 cup cold water

Melt butter over medium heat in saucepan. Add Basic White Sauce Mix and water. Bring to a boil, stirring constantly.
YIELDS: 1 cup

Medium White Sauce

2 tbsp. butter
⅓ cup Basic White Sauce Mix (see recipe)
¾ cup cold water

Melt butter over medium heat in saucepan. Add Basic White Sauce Mix and water. Bring to a boil, stirring constantly.
YIELDS: about 1 cup

Thick White Sauce

2 tbsp. butter
⅔ cup Basic White Sauce Mix (see recipe)
1 cup cold water

Melt butter over medium heat in saucepan. Add Basic White Sauce Mix and water. Bring to a boil, stirring constantly.
YIELDS: 1 cup

MARINADE

This sauce is simple to make and delivers a wonderful zest to all your meats.

⅓ cup lemon juice
½ cup olive or vegetable oil
2 cloves garlic
2 tsp. salt
⅓ tsp. black pepper

Place all ingredients in an electric blender and blend on high speed until puréed. Store in an airtight container in the refrigerator.

For lamb marinade: Add ½ tsp. rosemary.

For chicken marinade: Add ½ tsp. tarragon.

For pork marinade: Add ½ tsp. thyme.

YIELDS: 1 cup

SALAD DRESSINGS

BLEU CHEESE DRESSING #1

Yummy on hamburgers and as a tasty dip for chicken wings.

⅓ cup plain yogurt
⅔ cup mayonnaise
⅓ cup crumbled bleu cheese
1 tsp. Worcestershire sauce
Dash of garlic salt

Mix all ingredients together in a bowl until thoroughly blended. Refrigerate.
YIELDS: about 1⅓ cups

BLEU CHEESE DRESSING #2

Another great recipe for salads or for use as a vegetable dip.

2 cups sour cream
2 tbsp. mayonnaise
½ tsp. garlic
½ tsp. paprika
½ tsp. black pepper
2 tbsp. tarragon vinegar
¼ to ½ lb. crumbled bleu cheese

In a bowl, combine all ingredients except bleu cheese. Whip with a wire whisk until blended. Add crumbled bleu cheese and stir altogether. Chill before serving. Keep refrigerated.
YIELDS: about 3 cups

ROQUEFORT DRESSING

Top your cool, crisp salads with this rich and tangy dressing.

8 oz. cottage cheese
½ cup crumbled Roquefort cheese
Dash of Tabasco sauce
Dash of Worcestershire sauce
½ tsp. salt
Skim milk

In an electric blender, beat on high speed the cheeses, sauces, and salt until smooth and creamy. Thin with skim milk to desired consistency. Store in a tightly sealed container in the refrigerator. **YIELDS:** about 8 oz.

NO-MAYONNAISE RANCH DRESSING

Makes a great dipping sauce for cheese poppers or as a dressing for potato salad.

1 cup low-fat sour cream
½ cup buttermilk
½ tsp. dried parsley
½ tsp. dried chives
½ tsp. garlic powder
¼ tsp. dried dill weed or tarragon
¼ tsp. onion powder
⅛ tsp. black pepper

Combine all ingredients into a mixing bowl and whisk until smooth. Keep refrigerated in a covered container. Chill 30 minutes before serving. **YIELDS:** 12 oz.

BUTTERMILK DRESSING

Discover a new way to enjoy sweet potato fries with this exciting dressing.

½ cup mayonnaise
¼ cup sour cream
¼ cup buttermilk
2 tbsp. grated Parmesan cheese
½ tsp. dry mustard
¼ tsp. paprika
¼ tsp. celery seed
⅛ tsp. garlic powder

Combine all ingredients in a mixing bow. Stir until thoroughly blended. Store in a covered container in the refrigerator.

YIELDS: about 1¾ cups

DIETER'S SOUR CREAM SUBSTITUTE

How about a few spoonfuls of this dieter's delight on your next baked potato?

4 tbsp. skim milk
1 tbsp. lemon juice
¼ tsp. salt
1 cup low-fat cottage cheese

Combine all ingredients into the container of an electric blender. Beat on medium high until smooth and creamy. Place in a covered jar and keep refrigerated.

YIELDS: about 1 cup

COLESLAW DRESSING

This recipe is quick and easy to make. Try it as a seafood dip.

1 cup mayonnaise
1½ tbsp. prepared horseradish
2 tsp. sugar
1 tsp. onion powder
½ tsp. salt

Combine all ingredients and mix until well blended. Refrigerate.
YIELDS: about 1 cup

CREAMY COLESLAW DRESSING

Delicious mixed with shredded cabbage and carrots.

1 cup sour cream or plain yogurt
2 tbsp. vinegar
2 tsp. sugar
1 tsp. onion powder
1 tbsp. prepared horseradish

In a mixing bowl combine all ingredients together and stir until well blended. Refrigerate.
YIELDS: about 1 cup

FRENCH DRESSING MIX

Stock your pantry by making extra packets of this dressing. Then sit back and count the savings.

¼ cup sugar
1½ tsp. paprika
1 tsp. dry mustard
⅛ tsp. onion powder
Dash of cayenne pepper (optional)

Combine all ingredients together and store in an airtight zip-top bag. Keep in a cool, dry place.
YIELDS: 1 packet

FRENCH DRESSING

1 packet French Dressing Mix (see recipe)
¼ cup wine vinegar
¾ cup vegetable oil

To a glass jar with a lid, add French Dressing Mix, vinegar, and oil. Tightly seal lid and shake until mixture is thoroughly blended. Keep refrigerated.
YIELDS: about 1 cup

CREAMY FRENCH DRESSING
Substitute low-fat mayonnaise if you want to cut calories.

1 cup mayonnaise
1 tsp. dry mustard
½ tsp. garlic powder
1 tsp. paprika
2 tbsp. sugar
2 tbsp. cider vinegar

Combine all ingredients together. Stir until smooth and creamy. Keep in a closed container in the refrigerator.
YIELDS: about 1¼ cups

AVOCADO DIP
Holy Guacamole! I've had avocado dips in Mexican restaurants before, but this dip is the best yet.

2 large avocados
1 tbsp. lemon juice or lime juice
1¼ tsp. sugar
¼ tsp. garlic powder, to taste
Dash of onion powder
½ tsp. Tabasco sauce

Peel and mash avocados in a large bowl until partly smooth. Immediately add lemon juice and the balance of the ingredients. Blend thoroughly. Serve with chips.
YIELDS: about 12 oz.

ITALIAN DRESSING
Leave out the Romano cheese to turn this into a tasty marinade for meats.

¾ cup olive oil
⅓ cup wine vinegar
1½ tsp. sugar
¼ tsp. celery seeds
¼ tsp. ground basil
1 tsp. ground oregano
⅛ tsp. onion powder
¼ tsp. garlic powder
¼ tsp. parsley flakes
2 tsp. grated Romano cheese

Blend all ingredients together and pour into a glass jar with a tight-fitting lid. Refrigerate. Shake briskly before serving.
YIELDS: about 1 cup

WINE VINAIGRETTE DRESSING
This is a quality dressing made with the richness of olive oil.

¾ cup olive oil
½ cup wine vinegar
2 tsp. sugar
½ tsp. salt
½ tsp. tarragon
Dash of Tabasco sauce (optional)

Mix all ingredients together in a mixing bowl. Store in a tightly covered jar. Shake well before using.
YIELDS: about 1¼ cups

MAYONNAISE (BLENDER METHOD)

You can substitute half olive oil and half canola oil for the full measurement of canola oil.

2 egg yolks, pasteurized
1 tbsp. vinegar
¼ tsp. dry mustard
⅛ tsp. paprika
Dash of cayenne pepper (optional)
1 cup canola oil
1 tbsp. lemon juice

In an electric blender, thoroughly blend egg yolks, vinegar, dry mustard, paprika, and cayenne (optional). On slow speed, gradually pour in a ½ cup of the oil. Scrape inside of container as needed. Add lemon juice to mixture. Blend well. Once the emulsion reaches the proper consistency (it will look like mayonnaise and not separate), continue on slow speed while gradually adding the remaining oil. Blend until thoroughly mixed and smooth. Keep refrigerated.

YIELDS: about 1¼ cups

MAYONNAISE (MIXER METHOD)

This mayonnaise delivers a real homemade taste.

3 egg yolks, pasteurized
1 pinch dry mustard
¼ tsp. prepared mustard
¼ tsp. salt
2 cups canola oil
1 tbsp. water
1½ tbsp. cider vinegar
1½ tbsp. lemon juice
Dash of Worcestershire sauce

Note: Ingredients should be at room temperature. With an electric mixer, blend the first 4 ingredients at low speed. Slowly add 1 cup of oil, starting with just a drop at a time, mixing continuously. As the eggs and oil mix and thicken, increase the rate at which you add the oil. Once the emulsion reaches the proper consistency (it will look like mayonnaise and not separate), gradually add the water, vinegar, and remaining oil. Continue to mix until thoroughly blended. Stir in lemon juice and Worcestershire sauce. Taste and season with more lemon juice, salt, or pepper if desired. Keep refrigerated. Whip mayonnaise just before using.

YIELDS: about 2 cups

SOUR CREAM DRESSING

This dressing gives asparagus or green beans a lively taste.

2 tbsp. minced onions
1 tbsp. butter
1 tbsp. flour
1 tsp. sugar
½ tsp. salt
¾ cup or more of sour cream
1 tsp. vinegar

In a saucepan, sauté onions in butter until tender. Blend in flour, sugar, and salt, to taste. Slowly stir in sour cream and cook until thick. Add vinegar and stir to blend well. Keep refrigerated.
YIELDS: about ¾ cup

THOUSAND ISLAND DRESSING

To make Russian Dressing, use chili sauce instead of ketchup in the recipe.

1 cup mayonnaise
¼ cup ketchup
2 tbsp. sweet relish
2¼ tbsp. finely minced olives
1 pimento, finely minced
Juice of ½ lemon
Dash of Worcestershire sauce
Dash of Tabasco sauce

Thoroughly blend all ingredients together. Keep refrigerated.
YIELDS: about 1½ cups

CHEESES

COTTAGE CHEESE

¼ Junket Rennet Tablet
½ cup water
1 gallon skim milk
¼ cup cultured buttermilk
1 tsp. salt
⅓ cup cream

In a small bowl, dissolve rennet tablet in water. Set aside. In a 5-qt. stainless steel pot, heat skim milk and buttermilk to lukewarm. Add rennet tablet solution to pot and stir to blend. Cover and let set in a warm place for about 12 to 15 hours or until a firm curd forms. Cut curd into pieces measuring ½". Heat curd over hot water to a temperature of 110 degrees F for approximately 25 minutes, stirring every few minutes. (This process heats the curd throughout.) Pour curd into a colander lined with cheesecloth. The curd may be drained in the refrigerator lifted above a bowl to catch the drippings. This may take a couple of days. After whey has drained, lift the curd while still in cheesecloth and place in a pan of cold water for 1 to 2 minutes. Stir and press with a spoon. Immerse in a pan of ice water for 1 to 2 minutes. Return to colander and drain off whey completely. If cloth becomes clogged, lift the cloth back and scrape the curd away from the cloth. Add salt and cream. Keep refrigerated in a tightly closed container.
YIELDS: about 16 oz.

CREAM CHEESE (NEUFCHÂTEL)

Mixing cream cheese and garlic powder makes a spicy stuffing for celery.

1 gallon milk
¼ Junket Rennet Tablet
¼ cup cultured buttermilk
Salt to taste

Pour milk into a 5-qt. stainless steel pot and heat to lukewarm temperature, approximately 100 degrees F. In a small bowl, dissolve rennet table and water. Set aside. Add buttermilk to pot of warmed milk and then add dissolved rennet tablet solution. Thoroughly blend the mixture. Cover and let set overnight at room temperature (about 70 degrees F). When the curd begins to form, cut into ½" cubes. Ladle the curd and whey into a large strainer lined with a cheesecloth placed over a gallon-size bowl to catch the whey. If the cloth becomes clogged, lift the cloth back and scrape the curd away from the cloth. When most of the whey has drained through, lift the cloth by all 4 corners to drain overnight in the refrigerator. A shelf of the refrigerator would work just fine. The next day remove the cheese from the cloth and mix in salt according to taste. Keep covered in the refrigerator until ready to use.
YIELDS: about 12 oz.

STRAWBERRY CREAM CHEESE SPREAD

These blends are quite popular in grocery stores, but you can make it yourself for far less than you can purchase it prepared.

2 to 3 tbsp. strawberry preserves
1 8-oz. package cream cheese, softened

Hand mix the strawberry preserves and cream cheese in a bowl until thoroughly blended. Do not use an electric mixer. Store in a covered container in the refrigerator. This is delicious on your morning toast with coffee.
YIELDS: 8 oz.

PARMESAN CHEESE

I was so excited when I tasted the finished product; it is just like store bought.

2 qt. milk
1 Junket Rennet Tablet
¼ cup water
Salt

Pour milk into a large pot and heat to lukewarm. Remove from heat. In a small bowl, dissolve rennet tablet in water. Add to warmed milk and stir to blend well. Let set for about 30 minutes until a firm curd forms. Milk must be warm for a curd to form. With a knife, cut curd into small pieces, cutting diagonally and then horizontally. Drain curd from whey using a lined colander. This may take up to 2 days. Gather up the curd and gradually mold with hand, squeezing out whey until a ball is formed. Salt the ball of cheese with your hands. Continue to salt ball every day for a week. Wrap ball in a nylon net and hang in a cool place to drain. When cheese is thoroughly dry (may take several weeks) grate as needed. **Note:** Ageing this cheese 6 months or longer greatly improves the flavor. Keep in a cool, dry place tightly wrapped. YIELDS: about ½ lb.

BREADS

Biscuit Mix

Keep this bulk mix handy; it makes quick-and-easy country-style home-made biscuits.

8 cups all-purpose flour
4 tbsp. baking powder
3 tsp. salt
2 cups solid vegetable shortening

In a large bowl, sift flour, baking powder, and salt together. With a pastry blender cut in the shortening until mixture resembles tiny peas. Store in a tightly covered container in a cool, dry place.
YIELDS: about 10 cups

Homemade Biscuits

Nothing beats the taste of these country-style biscuits.

¾ cup milk or buttermilk
½ tsp. butter extract
1 tsp. sugar
2 cups Biscuit Mix (see recipe)

In a bowl, combine milk, extract, and sugar. Moisten Biscuit Mix with liquid using a fork to mix lightly. Turn dough onto lightly floured board. Knead gently. Roll out to ¾" thickness. Cut with floured round cutter. Place biscuits on an ungreased cookie sheet and bake in a 450-degree oven for about 10 to 15 minutes or until lightly browned.
YIELDS: about 12 small biscuits

BREADSTICKS

For delicious Italian-style breadsticks, roll dough in Parmesan cheese.

⅔ cup warm water
½ tsp. sugar
1 package dry yeast
2 tbsp. olive oil
1 tsp. salt
2 cups all-purpose flour

In a bowl, mix water, sugar, and yeast. Let set for 10 minutes. Add oil, salt, and 1 cup of flour and beat 4 minutes. Knead in the remaining 1 cup of flour and work dough until smooth and elastic in texture. Form dough into a ball and place in a greased bowl. Turn once. Cover and let rise until doubled in size. Punch down and divide dough into 32 pieces. Knead each piece into ropes 7" long. Place on a greased baking sheet to rise until doubled in size. Bake in a 325-degree oven for about 25 minutes or until done.
YIELDS: 32 sticks

PLAIN CRACKERS

Turn these into expensive gourmet crackers by sprinkling on your favorite seasonings before baking.

2 cups warm milk
4 tbsp. melted butter
2 tsp. baking powder
6 cups all-purpose flour
1 tsp. baking soda

Blend all ingredients together, adding additional milk or flour to make a workable dough. Knead dough until smooth. Roll out onto a lightly floured board to ⅛" thick and cut into desired shapes. Prick with a fork. Place on greased baking sheets. Bake in a 325-degree oven allowing crackers to rise as they bake. This recipe may be cut in half.

For Saltine Crackers, sprinkle with salt after dough has been shaped, then bake as directed.

YIELDS: about 2 lb.

GRAHAM CRACKERS

Quality ingredients add to the homemade taste of these honey-filled crackers.

½ cup evaporated milk
2 tbsp. lemon juice
1 cup dark brown sugar
½ cup honey
1 cup vegetable oil
2 tsp. vanilla extract
2 eggs, beaten
6 cups graham flour
1 tsp. baking soda
1 tsp. salt

In a large bowl, combine milk and lemon juice. In a separate bowl, blend sugar, honey, oil, vanilla extract, and eggs and add to liquid mixture. Add graham flour, baking soda, and salt and mix. Divide mixture into 4 parts. Roll each part out on greased and floured cookie sheets to ⅛" thickness. Prick with fork and bake in a 375-degree oven until lightly browned, about 15 minutes. Cut immediately into squares when removed from oven.

YIELDS: about 2 lb.

HOMEMADE BREADCRUMBS

1 loaf of day-old sliced bread

Toast bread in toaster and lay flat on the counter top to dry and harden. Crush bread by hand for stuffings. Put in a zip-type bag and mash with a pastry roller for a finer texture for coating meats. Be sure all the air is pressed out of the bag and the end is closed tightly to prevent crumbs from falling out. Other breads like bagels, English muffins, cornbread, and even plain, dried cornflakes can be used for making breadcrumbs. Store in an airtight container in a cool, dry place and label.

YIELDS: 20 oz.

ITALIAN-STYLE BREADCRUMBS

This is a good way to use up all that left over bread.

2 cups breadcrumbs (use slices of day-old bread toasted, air dried, and grated)
1 tsp. onion powder
1 tbsp. dried parsley flakes
1 tsp. seasoned salt
½ tsp. pepper
1 tbsp. Italian Seasoning (see recipe)
1 tsp. garlic powder
1 tsp. dried ground basil
¼ cup grated Parmesan cheese (optional)

Combine all ingredients together in an airtight container and store in a cool, dry place until ready to use. The number of bread slices needed to equal 2 cups varies with the breads used. You can also use day-old bagels, English muffins, or sourdough bread to help equal 2 cups.

YIELDS: 2¼ cups

CROUTONS

You will always have plenty of croutons for your salads when you see how easy it is to make them.

1 loaf of day-old bread (any type will work)
Garlic Butter (see recipe)

Toast bread. Let dry completely on counter. Cut into cubes using an electric knive. Melt Garlic Butter in frying pan and sauté croutons to coat evenly. Remove to cool and dry. Keep in an airtight container.

BASIC CORNBREAD MIX

1 cup all-purpose flour
2 tsp. baking powder
½ tsp. baking soda
2 tbsp. sugar
1 tsp. salt
1 cup cornmeal
2 tbsp. solid vegetable shortening

Sift first 6 ingredients together into a large bowl. Cut in shortening with a pastry blender until mixture is a fine texture like tiny peas. Store in an airtight package, such as a zip-type plastic bag, in a cool, dry place.
YIELDS: 1 packet

COUNTRY CORNBREAD

There's nothing like the richness of real buttermilk to bring out that country cornbread taste.

2 eggs, slightly beaten
1 cup milk or buttermilk
1 packet Basic Cornbread Mix (see recipe)

In a bowl, whisk eggs and milk and add to mix. Stir gently until well blended. Do not beat. Pour into a greased and floured loaf pan. Bake in a 425-degree oven for about 25 minutes or until done.
YIELDS: 1 loaf

DATE NUT BREAD

The rich combination of dates and nuts makes this delicious bread a natural partner with coffee.

1 cup finely chopped dates
1 cup boiling water
½ stick butter, softened
½ cup dark brown sugar
¼ cup sugar
1 egg, beaten
1¾ cups all-purpose flour
½ tsp. salt
½ tsp. baking powder
½ tsp. baking soda
¾ cup chopped pecans or walnuts

Add dates to boiling water and let set. In a large bowl, beat butter and sugars until creamy. Add egg and continue to beat until well blended. Mix in liquid from dates. Gradually beat in sifted flour, salt, baking powder, and baking soda until creamy.

Stir in dates and chopped nuts. Pour into a greased and floured loaf pan and bake in a 350-degree oven for about 45 minutes or until a toothpick inserted in the center comes out dry.

YIELDS: 1 loaf

FRENCH BREAD

This is the real thing. Hot French bread from your oven costs so little to make.

7 to 8 cups all-purpose flour
5 tbsp. sugar
1 tbsp. salt
3 packages yeast
3 tbsp. melted butter
2½ cups warm water
Corn oil
Cornmeal
2 egg whites, slightly beaten

Mix 4 cups flour, sugar, salt, and yeast in a large bowl. Gradually add melted butter and warm water. Stir to blend. Slowly add remaining flour, working in with each cup. Knead dough until elastic and smooth. Divide into 4 pieces. Roll out each piece into an 8"x15" rectangle and begin to roll tightly as you would if making a jellyroll. Grease 4 pans and shape dough into pans. Brush tops of bread with corn oil and drizzle with cornmeal. Let rise until doubled in size. Brush with egg whites and place in a 375-degree oven until done and bread is a beautiful golden brown. (I purchased twin French bread loaf pans at a large retail store. The pans really help hold the narrow shape of the loaves when baking.)

YIELDS: 4 loaves

Hamburger Buns

Make these into small sizes and you'll have minature hamburgers to serve at parties.

5½ to 7 cups all-purpose flour
⅓ cup nonfat dry milk
¼ cup sugar
2 packages yeast
1 tbsp. salt
⅓ cup melted margarine
2 cups warm water

Mix 2 cups flour, dry milk, sugar, yeast, and salt in large bowl. Add margarine and water. Beat 2 minutes with electric mixer. Add 1 cup flour and continue to beat. Gradually add enough remaining flour to form a workable dough. Remove from bowl and knead on lightly floured board until smooth and elastic in texture. Place in greased bowl, turning once, and cover. Let rise until doubled in size. Punch down and let rise again until less than doubled. Divide dough in half and divide each half into 10 pieces. Form each piece into a round ball. Grease pan and place balls about 2" apart, pressing each one down to flatten. Cover and let rise until doubled in size. Bake in a 375-degree oven for about 15 to 20 minutes or until done. Cool completely then slice.
Yields: about 20 buns

Melba Toast

Melba toast is so expensive in the stores that I never buy them. Now you can make your own and serve them often. Top with your favorite cheese.

Slice your favorite homemade wheat bread extra thin. Place on top oven rack and bake at 200 degrees until crisp and dry. When cool, stack in an airtight container. Store in a dry place.

Yeast Bread

Once you have tasted yeast bread, you will never want to buy another loaf of sliced bread from the grocery store again.

½ cup sugar
2 tsp. salt
2 packages yeast
½ cup warm milk
1½ cups warm water
¼ cup melted butter
6 to 7 cups all-purpose flour, or 3½ cups wheat flour and
   3½ cups white flour
1 egg, beaten

In a large bowl, combine sugar, salt, yeast, milk, water, and butter. Stir well to blend. Let set 2 minutes. Add 4 cups all-purpose flour (or 2 cups wheat flour and 2 cups white flour) and egg. Beat well. Gradually work in remaining flour or enough to knead dough until smooth and elastic. Place in a greased bowl. Turn over once and cover bowl. Set in a warm place. Let rise until doubled. Punch down, cover, and let rise again, about 30 minutes. Punch down and shape into rolls or loaves. Place in greased pans to rise until doubled in size. Bake in a 350-degree oven until lightly browned.
Yields: 20 rolls or 2 loaves

Pizza Dough

A taste of Italy comes to your home! Create delicious miniature pizzas for a fraction of the cost of store-bought brands.

1 package yeast
1 cup warm water
2½ cups all-purpose flour
2 tbsp. vegetable oil
1 tsp. sugar
1 tsp. salt

In a large bowl, add yeast to warm water and stir to dissolve. Let set 2 minutes. Add remaining ingredients. Knead dough, adding extra flour, if needed, to form a workable dough. Let rest 5 minutes. Punch down and roll dough on lightly floured board to the shape of your pizza pans.
YIELDS: 2 crusts

BUTTER

Pecan Butter

This is a gourmet butter that adds a rich quality taste to pancakes, biscuits, and breads.

¼ cup butter, softened
¼ cup finely minced almonds
⅛ tsp. pecan extract

Combine all ingredients together in a small mixing bowl and stir until well blended. Store in a closed container in the refrigerator.
Yields: about ½ cup

Maple Butter

This butter says "country home." It is a perfect match for pancakes, waffles, and homemade biscuits.

½ cup butter, softened
¼ cup pure maple syrup

In a mixing bowl, beat together the butter and maple syrup until mixture is fluffy and well blended. Store in a closed container in the refrigerator.
Yields: about ¾ cup

Orange Butter

Try this full-flavored butter on warmed English breakfast muffins, or use in your cookie mix recipe. It's so good you'll want to eat it by itself.

½ cup butter, softened
1 tbsp orange juice
1 tsp. grated orange peel

In a mixing bowl, add all ingredients and stir until well blended. Store in a closed container in the refrigerator.
Yields: ½ cup

PEPPERMINT BUTTER

This butter is absolutely wonderful on dinner rolls or cinnamon-raisin bagels.

½ cup unsalted butter, softened
1 tbsp. confectioners' sugar
½ tsp. peppermint extract

In a mixing bowl, cream together butter and confectioners' sugar. Add extract and stir mixture until well blended. Store in an airtight container in the refrigerator.

YIELDS: ½ cup

GARLIC BUTTER

Spread this delicious herbed butter generously on thinly sliced French bread and broil in the oven. It is the perfect partner to any cooked pasta dish.

½ cup butter, softened
2 tbsp. grated Parmesan cheese
½ tsp. garlic powder or 1 clove garlic, finely minced

Stir all ingredients together until well blended. Store in a closed container in the refrigerator.

YIELDS: about ½ cup

Pizza Butter

This special blend of herbs and cheeses turns ordinary breads into an Italian art.

¾ cup butter, softened
1 6-oz. can tomato paste
1 tsp. ground oregano
1 tsp. ground basil
⅛ tsp. garlic powder
8 oz. shredded mozzarella cheese
6 oz. shredded cheddar cheese
½ tsp. sugar

Combine all ingredients in a large bowl and stir until mixture is thoroughly blended. Store in a covered container and keep refrigerated.

Yields: about 3 cups

For Miniature Pizzas, spread butter on split English muffins and broil in the oven until slightly browned and bubbly. Minced sandwich pepperoni can also be added to the tops of each muffin before broiling.

MAIN DISHES

SLOPPY JOE SEASONING MIX

Make extra packages for quick-to-fix suppers.

1 tsp. onion powder
1 tsp. cornstarch
1 tsp. salt
½ tsp. sugar
¼ tsp. chili powder
1 tsp. dried bell pepper flakes
½ tsp. garlic powder
¼ tsp. celery seed
¼ tsp. dry mustard
Dash black pepper

Mix all ingredients together. Seal in a small zip-top bag in a cool, dry place. Use for making Sloppy Joe Sandwiches.
YIELDS: 1 packet

SLOPPY JOE SANDWICHES

Gather the family tonight for this delicious supper made fresh, not from the can.

1 lb. ground meat
1 packet Sloppy Joe Seasoning Mix (see recipe)
1 cup water
1 6-oz. can tomato paste
6 buns

Brown meat in a skillet and drain fat. Stir in Sloppy Joe Seasoning Mix, water, and tomato paste. Cover and simmer 20 minutes. Serve hot on buns.
YIELDS: 6 servings

CORN DOG #1

Kids love corn dogs, and this recipe combines simple ingredients to keep the supply coming.

1 cup cornmeal
1 cup all-purpose flour
2 tbsp. sugar
2 tsp. baking powder
½ tsp. salt
1 egg, slightly beaten
1 cup milk
2 tbsp. melted butter
10 hot dogs
Skewers
Vegetable oil

Sift all dry ingredients together in a mixing bowl. Add beaten egg and milk. Blend in the melted butter. Mix well. Pour mixture into a deep container. Skewer each hot dog and dip into the batter. Roll or pat lightly with cornmeal or flour. Deep fry in vegetable oil. Drain on paper towels.
YIELDS: 10 corn dogs

Corn Dog #2 (quick fix)

You will never pay the high cost of frozen corn dogs again. Enjoy the quality and the savings.

1 package Jiffy Corn Muffin Mix
1 egg, beaten
⅓ cup water
10 hot dogs
Skewers
Vegetable oil

In a mixing bowl, combine dry corn muffin mix, beaten egg, and water and mix by hand just until blended. Pour mixture into a large and deep tumbler. Insert skewers into ends of hot dogs. Hold hot dog by the stick and, with a twirling motion, dip into the batter until evenly coated. Pat or roll into dry cornmeal or flour. Deep fry in vegetable oil until done. Drain on paper towels.
YIELDS: 10 corn dogs

Baked Beans

The molasses and brown sugar give this recipe a sensational flavor.

1 lb. navy beans, cooked
1 onion, finely chopped
½ tsp. garlic powder
½ cup brown sugar
¼ cup molasses
½ tsp. salt
Pieces of cooked bacon
1 15-oz. can tomato sauce or ketchup

In an ovenware bowl, combine all ingredients. Drizzle extra brown sugar and molasses on top. Bake in a 375-degree oven for about 30 minutes.
YIELDS: 6 servings

Chili Seasoning Mix

This has the same quality as the name brands but costs a whole lot less.

2 tbsp. chili seasoning
2 tsp. ground oregano
2 tsp. ground cumin
1 tsp. salt
3 tbsp. dried onion flakes
½ tsp. red pepper flakes
1 tsp. cayenne pepper

Combine all ingredients together and store in an airtight package, such as a zip-type plastic bag. Keep in a cool, dry place. Use for making Homemade Chili.
Yields: 1 packet

Homemade Chili

There's nothing like this warm and comforting chili on a cold, rainy day.

2 lb. lean ground meat
2 15-oz. cans tomato sauce or 1 6-oz. can diced tomatoes
    and 1 6-oz. can tomato sauce
1 packet Chili Seasoning Mix (see recipe)
15 oz. can navy or pinto beans (optional)

Brown meat in a saucepan until completely cooked. Drain off excess fat. Add tomato sauce and 1 packet of chili mix. Add canned beans, if desired. Stir on medium heat until blended. Reduce heat to simmer on low for about 1 hour.
Yields: 8 servings

BEEF JERKY

This is the oven method, but you may also use a food dehydrator. Both work quite well.

3 lb. lean beef
½ cup soy sauce
½ cup Worcestershire sauce
2 tsp. flavor enhancer
2 tsp. seasoned salt
2 tsp. onion powder
⅔ tsp. garlic powder
⅔ tsp. black pepper

Slice beef as thin as possible into ⅜" wide strips. In a large bowl, combine remaining ingredients. Stir until all spices are dissolved. Place meat in marinade, making sure beef is completely covered with sauce. Marinate overnight in the refrigerator, turning if necessary. In the morning, line the bottom of oven rack with foil to hold drippings. Lay strips on oven rack and cook at 150 degrees (or lowest setting) for at least 8 hours or until meat's appearance is of dry leather. The longer the beef cooks, the crispier it becomes. Whatever the time, be sure the meat is completely cooked! Store in an airtight container in a cool, dry place. If moisture forms inside the container, do not eat.

YIELDS: about 30 strips

BEEF RICE SEASONING MIX

Packaging it yourself saves you money every time.

1½ cups uncooked long-grain rice
2 tbsp. instant beef bouillon or 6 cubes crushed
½ tsp. dried tarragon
¾ tsp. onion powder
1½ tsp. dried parsley flakes
¾ tsp. garlic powder
½ tsp. dried basil

Pour rice into a small plastic bag. Combine all the seasonings together, wrap in a piece of aluminum foil, and then place it inside the plastic bag with the rice. Label. Store in a cool, dry place. Use for making Beef Rice.
YIELDS: 1 packet

BEEF RICE

The rich robust flavor in this dish is sure to please the family.

2 tbsp. butter or margarine
1 packet Beef Rice Seasoning Mix (see recipe)
3½ cups water

In a large skillet, melt butter. Remove rice from package and add to skillet with the butter. Lightly brown the rice in butter, stirring often to prevent burning. Add water and the seasonings from the foil packet. Stir to a boil. Lower heat and cover for about 10 minutes. Remove cover and continue heating until liquid is absorbed and rice is soft and tender. Add additional water for a more moist texture.
YIELDS: about 7½ cups

Beef Stew Seasoning Mix

The name-brand imitation of this mix is expensive in the grocery store. Now you can drastically cut the cost by packaging your own Beef Stew Seasoning Mix for pennies.

1 tsp. instant beef bouillon
2 tsp. salt
1 bay leaf, crushed
½ tsp. thyme
½ tsp. rosemary
½ tsp. oregano
½ tsp. onion powder
½ tsp. garlic powder
½ cup all-purpose flour

Combine all the ingredients together and store in an airtight package, such as a zip-type bag. Store in a cool, dry place. Use for making Beef Stew.
Yields: 1 packet

Beef Stew

This delicious stew is easy to make and perfectly seasoned. Serve with cooked rice for a full-bodied meal for a hungry family.

2 lb. lean stew meat
3 tbsp. vegetable oil
1 packet Beef Stew Seasoning Mix (see recipe)
4½ cups water
6 carrots, peeled and diced
4 to 5 medium potatoes, peeled and diced

In a large pot, brown meat in vegetable oil and remove fat drippings. Add Beef Stew Mix and water. Stir until seasonings are well blended and bring to a boil. Reduce heat. Cover and simmer,

stirring occasionally for 1½ hours or until meat is completely done. Add diced carrots and potatoes and cook ½ hour longer or until vegetables are tender. Add additional water if necessary.
YIELDS: 6 servings

CHICKEN RICE SEASONING MIX

1½ cups uncooked long-grain rice
2 tbsp. chicken bouillon or 6 cubes crushed
½ tsp. dried tarragon
¾ tsp. garlic power
¾ tsp. onion powder
1½ tsp. dried parsley flakes

Pour rice into a small, plastic, airtight bag. Combine the seasonings and wrap in aluminum foil. Place foil packet inside the plastic bag with the rice. Label. Use for making Chicken Rice.
YIELDS: 1 packet

CHICKEN RICE

This recipe makes a family-size meal. Serve with a crisp salad and green beans.

2 tbsp. butter or margarine
1 packet Chicken Rice Seasoning Mix (see recipe)
3½ cups water

In a large skillet, sauté butter and the rice from the package. Heat on high. When lightly browned, add water and seasoning mix. Bring to a boil. Lower heat and cover about 10 minutes or until rice is tender and liquid is absorbed. Add additional water if you want a more moist texture.
YIELDS: 4 servings

Low-Fat Chicken and Rice Soup

This low fat soup is soothing and very nutritious. It's definitely a healthy choice.

4 cups low-sodium chicken broth
1 small onion, finely chopped
2 ribs celery
1 cup sliced mushrooms (optional)
½ cup uncooked rice
2 cups diced cooked chicken

To a large saucepan on medium heat, add broth and all the vegetables. Bring to a boil and add rice. Simmer for 20 minutes until rice is tender. Add cooked chicken and continue to simmer for about 5 minutes.
Yields: 4 servings

Cream of Chicken Soup

Half-and-half and a special blend of spices adds quality and richness to this soup.

¼ cup butter
¼ tsp. onion powder
¼ tsp. garlic powder
¼ tsp. poultry seasoning
¼ cup all-purpose flour
½ cup whole milk
½ cup half-and-half
3 cups chicken broth
1½ cups diced cooked chicken

In a saucepan on medium heat, melt butter. Add all ingredients except cooked chicken. With a wire whisk, whip mixture until thoroughly blended and smooth. Cook on medium-high heat until slightly thickened. Reduce heat to simmer. Stir often to prevent sticking. Add chicken. For a lighter cream soup with less fat and calories, substitute skim milk for half-and-half.

YIELDS: 4 servings

CREAM OF BROCCOLI SOUP

This delicious soup is bathed with the richness of real chedder cheese.

½ cup chopped onions
¼ cup butter
¼ cup all-purpose flour
3 cups water
4 tsp. instant chicken bouillon
2 10-oz. packages frozen broccoli, thawed and drained
3 cups shredded cheddar cheese
2 cups half-and-half

In a large saucepan, sauté chopped onions in butter until tender. Stir in the flour and gradually add the water to achieve a well-blended texture. Add the bouillon and broccoli. Continue cooking until mixture is thickened and broccoli is tender. In a separate bowl, combine the cheddar cheese with the half-and-half and stir mixture into the large saucepan with the broccoli. Heat until cheese is melted and blended well.

YIELDS: 4 servings

Cup of Soup Mix

A quick-to-fix soup that can travel anywhere.

1 tsp. instant beef or chicken bouillon
1½ tsp. dried onion flakes
½ tsp. dried parsley
⅓ cup egg noodles, cracked into small pieces

Combine all ingredients and store in a tightly sealed packet.
YIELDS: 1 packet

Cup of Soup

Add shredded cheese, diced meats, or chopped mushrooms for a creative change to an old standby.

1 cup of boiling water
1 packet Cup of Soup Mix (see recipe)

In a small saucepan, add water and soup mix. Bring mixture to a boil. Cover and let simmer for 5 minutes or until noodles are tender. Add shredded cheese, diced meats, or chopped mushrooms for a creative change to an old standby.
YIELDS: 1 serving

CREAMY TOMATO SOUP

Create your own taste sensation by adding a topping of shredded cheese to your soup bowl.

1 28-oz. can crushed tomatoes
2 cups chicken broth
2 tbsp. unsalted butter
2 tbsp. sugar
1 tbsp. chopped onion
1 tsp. dried parsley
1 tbsp. tomato paste
Several sprigs of fresh sweet basil (optional)
2 cups light cream

In a large saucepan, mix all the ingredients together except the cream. Simmer 1 hour. Heat and stir cream in a separate pot for 1 or 2 minutes. Add hot cream to hot tomato soup and stir. Salt to taste. YIELDS: about 8 servings (⅞ cup each)

CREAMY MACARONI AND CHEESE

This is a basic recipe for macaroni and cheese. Use more or less cheese to suit your taste.

1½ cups elbow macaroni
4 cups water
1½ tsp. salt
½ cup milk
3 tbsp. butter
½ cup grated Velveeta cheese
⅓ cup grated mozzarella cheese

Add uncooked macaroni to 4 cups salted, boiling water. Cook until tender. Drain in a colander. In a large saucepan, combine milk, butter, and cheeses and heat on low until all ingredients are thoroughly blended. Add drained macaroni and stir until evenly coated.

YIELDS: 8 servings (½ cup each)

EGG PASTA

Pasta never tasted so good when you make it fresh and ready to serve within the hour.

3 cups all-purpose, durum wheat, or semolina flour
3 eggs
¾ tsp. salt
2½ tsp. olive oil
Lukewarm water

In a large bowl, sift flour and form a mound. Make a well in the center of the mound and add eggs, salt, and olive oil (if using a food processor just add all the ingredients together in the container). Mix until well blended. Add water as needed to make a stiff but workable dough. Knead dough on floured surface until smooth. Let rest, covered, for 15 minutes. Divide dough in half. At this point, you can either cut by hand in various shapes or use a pasta machine. Dust the cut pasta with flour to keep from sticking. To cook immediately, shake off the excess flour and drop into a large pot of boiling, salted water. Cook until done. If you want to store it for later use, simply shape and separate the pasta and let dry overnight. Store in an airtight container or large zip-top bag.

YIELDS: about 1 lb.

CREOLE-FRIED FISH

This mouth-watering dish has all the right seasonings for a great cookout party.

2 tbsp. Creole Seafood Fish Fry Mix (see recipe)
½ cup all-purpose flour
½ cup cornmeal
Catfish, trout, tilapia, or try your local favorites
Cooking oil

Combine the Fish Fry Mix with flour and cornmeal in a shallow dish and mix well. Coat fish in the mixture. Dust off excess flour and pan fry in hot oil until golden brown.
YIELDS: enough batter to fry several lb. of fish

HUSH PUPPY SEASONING MIX

Make several of these packages and stock them in your pantry.

1 cup yellow cornmeal
1 cup all-purpose flour
2 tsp. baking powder
1 tbsp. sugar
1 tsp. lemon pepper
½ tsp. garlic powder
1 tsp. onion powder

Sift all ingredients together twice and store in a plastic airtight bag in a cool, dry place. Label. Use for making Hush Puppies.
YIELDS: 1 packet

Hush Puppies

These hush puppies are delicious. Try them with a honey mustard dip.

1 packet Hush Puppy Seasoning Mix (see recipe)
1 egg, beaten
¾ cup buttermilk

Mix all ingredients together in a bowl until thoroughly blended. Spoon into a hot skillet of vegetable oil and deep fry until golden brown, turning once. Drain on absorbent paper towels. Great with any seafood.
YIELDS: about 2 dozen

Meat Pot Pies

These delicious meat pies are packed with lots of fresh veggies and meat. There are no fillers here.

2 10¾-oz. cans cream of chicken soup
2 cups diced cooked chicken, turkey, or chopped beef
1 cup small early peas, cooked and drained
1 cup carrots, cooked and drained
3 unbaked pie shells, top and bottom

In a large mixing bowl, combine undiluted soup, meat, peas, and carrots and stir until completely blended. Spoon into individual pie shells and cover with pastry. Seal edges with fork and make slits in tops. Bake in a 375- to 400-degree oven for about 35 minutes or until lightly browned.
YIELDS: 3 pot pies

PORK SAUSAGE

The natural fresh taste of this pure pork sausage has no fillers or harmful additives.

2 lb. lean fresh pork
1 medium green bell pepper
1 medium onion
¼ cup firmly packed brown sugar
2 tbsp. soy sauce
1½ tsp. seasoned salt
1 tsp. garlic salt
½ tsp. cayenne pepper
½ tsp. poultry seasoning
Dash of black pepper

Place pork, green bell pepper, and onion in a meat grinder and grind together to a fine consistency. Place in a large bowl and add the balance of the ingredients. Mix well. Wrap into 2 rolls, or wrap pork into individual patties using layers of wax paper between each patty. Freeze or refrigerate until ready to use. Fry in a skillet until done before serving.

YIELDS: 8 servings

DIRTY RICE

The ground pork and special blend of savory spices make this a famous dish in the South.

1 lb. seasoned pork sausage
1 14-oz. can chicken broth
½ cup uncooked long-grain rice
1 tsp. dried minced onion
½ tsp. garlic powder

In a large, skillet brown pork sausage until well done. Drain off the grease. Stir in the chicken broth, rice, onion, and garlic. Simmer, covered, for about 15 minutes or until rice is tender and most of the broth is absorbed. Add additional water or broth for a more moist mixture.

YIELDS: 4 SERVINGS

SPANISH RICE SEASONING MIX

1 cup uncooked long-grain rice
½ tsp. dried basil
1 tsp. garlic powder
1 tsp. onion powder
2 tsp. parsley flakes
1 tsp. dried pepper flakes
2 tsp. chili powder
Dash cayenne pepper

Combine all ingredients together and store in a small, airtight, zip-type bag in a cool, dry place. Label. Use for making Spanish Rice.

YIELDS: 1 packet

SPANISH RICE

1 packet Spanish Rice Seasoning Mix (see recipe)
2 cups water
1 6-oz. can Rotel Diced Tomatoes and Green Chiles
1 tbsp. butter

Combine all ingredients in a large saucepan or deep skillet. Stir often. Bring mixture to a boil and reduce heat. Cover. Cook for 15 minutes or until rice is tender. Add additional water if you prefer the mixture to be more moist.

YIELDS: 4 servings

Seasoning Mix for Stuffing

½ tsp. dried marjoram
2 tsp. onion powder
1 tbsp. dried parsley flakes
¾ tsp. salt
½ tsp. dried basil
¼ tsp. dried thyme
¼ tsp. black pepper
1 tsp. garlic powder
1 tsp. dried celery flakes
2 tsp. chicken or beef bouillon or 3 cubes crushed

Mix all ingredients together and store in an airtight plastic bag or wrap tightly in aluminum foil and place in a container. Label. Use for making Poultry Stuffing.
Yields: 1 packet

Poultry Stuffing

½ stick butter
2 cups water
1 packet Seasoning Mix for Stuffing (see recipe)
4 cups Homemade Breadcrumbs (see recipe)
1 egg, beaten

In a saucepan, heat butter, water, and seasoning packet and bring to a boil. Reduce heat. Simmer and cover for 5 minutes. Stir in breadcrumbs and egg. Blend well. Add additional water if needed to obtain a more moist texture.
Yields: 4 cups

PASTRIES, FROSTINGS, AND CAKES

BAKING POWDER

Use this recipe when you run out of baking powder and save a trip to the market.

2 tsp. cream of tartar
1 tsp. baking soda
½ tsp. salt
½ tsp. cornstarch

In a bowl, sift all ingredients together 2 times. Store in an airtight container in a cool, dry place. Use in recipes that call for baking powder.

BROWN SUGAR

You can make brown sugar for about half of what it costs at the grocery store.

1 cup white sugar
2 tbsp. light or dark molasses

Blend sugar and molasses together in a bowl. Store in an airtight container in a cool, dry place.
YIELDS: about ½ cup

Self-Rising Flour

With this helpful recipe, you will never run out of self-rising flour again.

8 cups all-purpose flour
5 tbsp. baking powder
2 tbsp. sugar
1 tbsp. salt

Sift all ingredients together and store in an airtight container in a cool, dry place. Date and label.
Yields: 5 cups

Cake Flour

Forgot to get cake flour for your recipe? Here's the secret substitute that works.

3½ cups all-purpose flour
½ cup cornstarch

Combine both ingredients in a mixing bowl. Sift 2 times. Store in a tightly closed container in a cool, dry place. Label and date. Use within 6 months. This flour can be used in recipes that call for cake flour.
Yields: 4 cups

APPLE TURNOVERS

There is no comparison to the fresh taste of these hot turnovers.

¾ cup sugar
1 tbsp. cornstarch
¼ tsp. ground cloves
1½ tsp. ground cinnamon
5 cups apples (about 3 to 4 large apples), peeled, cored, and
    sliced thin
1 tbsp. lemon juice
4 prepared pie crusts or 4 homemade Pie Crusts (see recipe)

In a large bowl, combine sugar, cornstarch, cloves, and cinnamon with a wire whisk. Add apples and lemon juice. Toss well. Roll dough out on a lightly floured board to ⅛" thick. Cut into 6" circles. Place about ⅓ cup of the filling on half of each circle, staying ½" from the edges. Fold over and seal edge with a fork. Bake on greased cookie sheets at 425 degrees for about 15 minutes or until lightly browned.

YIELDS: 12 turnovers

JELLY DOUGHNUTS

When I first made these, I could not believe how perfect they came out. They were better than bakery bought and much less expensive.

1 package yeast
¼ cup warm water
1 cup warm milk
⅓ cup sugar
1 tsp. salt
⅓ cup butter, melted
3 eggs, beaten
5½ to 6½ cups all-purpose flour
Vegetable oil
32 oz. jar jelly (your favorite flavor)
Confectioners' sugar

Dissolve yeast in warm water in a bowl. Let rest 2 minutes. Add milk, sugar, salt, and butter to yeast mixture. Add eggs and stir well to blend. Gradually add enough flour to form a smooth workable dough. Knead on a lightly floured board until smooth and elastic. Divide into 3 parts. Roll out each part to ¼" thick. Cut into 3" circles. Place on greased cookie sheets. Let rise in warm place to double in size. Deep fry in hot vegetable oil until golden brown, turning once. Drain on absorbent paper towels. Let cool. Cut a small hole in side of doughnut and insert jelly to center using a pastry bag and wide, plain pastry tube. For powdered doughnuts, coat with confectioners' sugar.

YIELDS: about 3 dozen doughnuts

CINNAMON ROLLS

Incomparable in taste and quality at a savings that will amaze you.

1 package yeast
¼ cup warm water
¾ cup warm milk
¼ cup sugar
1 tsp. salt
¼ cup butter, melted
1 egg, beaten
3 to 3½ cups all-purpose flour
1¼ cups Cinnamon Mixture (see recipe)

Dissolve yeast in warm water. Let rest 2 minutes. Add milk, sugar, salt, and melted butter and mix until well blended. Add egg. Gradually work in the flour to form a pliable soft dough. Knead dough for about 10 minutes. Add additional flour or milk, if needed, to make dough smooth and elastic. Roll out on a lightly floured board to 10"x15" rectangle. Spread Cinnamon Mixture over dough and begin to roll from long side as in the style of a jellyroll. Pinch seam to seal. Cut into ¾" wide pieces (an electric knife works best). Place on greased cookie sheets, cut side down, and press lightly to flatten. Let rise until doubled. Bake in a 350-degree oven for about 20 to 25 minutes or until done. If desired, glaze when completely cooled (see Cinnamon Glaze recipe).

YIELDS: about 1½ dozen rolls

CINNAMON MIXTURE

The perfect blend of spices and raisins to complement your homemade cinnamon rolls.

1½ tsp. cinnamon
¾ cup sugar
½ cup raisins

Combine all ingredients and use as filling for Cinnamon Rolls.
YIELDS: enough for 1½ dozen rolls

CREAM PUFFS

It's like having your own bakery at home. The quality and taste are superb.

1 cup boiling water
½ cup butter
1 cup self-rising flour
4 eggs

In a saucepan, melt butter in boiling water. Lower heat and add flour. Stir well until ball forms and leaves the edges of the pot. Remove from heat and add eggs, one at a time, beating in after each addition. Drop by heaping teaspoonfuls on a greased cookie sheet. Bake in a 450-degree oven for about 15 minutes, then 20 minutes at 325 degrees or until done. When cool, slit and fill (see recipe for Cream Puff Filling). Sprinkle tops with powdered confectioners' sugar.
YIELDS: about 15 puffs

CREAM PUFF FILLING

A smooth creamy filling with no additives or preservatives.

½ cup sugar
⅓ cup all-purpose flour
½ tsp. salt
2 cups milk
2 eggs, beaten
1 tsp. vanilla extract

Mix sugar, flour, and salt in a saucepan. On medium heat, slowly stir in milk and cook until thickened. In a separate bowl, add a little of the hot mixture to eggs and vanilla until blended. Add egg mixture to the saucepan and return to heat until it boils. Stir constantly throughout this process to prevent sticking and burning. Cool. Use to fill Cream Puffs.

YIELDS: enough for about 15 puffs

GRAHAM PIE CRUST

You may enjoy using crushed chocolate cookies instead of graham crackers for an altogether different taste.

1½ cups graham cracker crumbs
¼ cup sugar
¼ cup butter, melted

In a mixing bowl, combine all ingredients until well blended. Press mixture into bottom and ½" up sides of pie pan. Bake in a 350-degree oven for about 8 minutes. This recipe can be easily doubled.

YIELDS: 1 pie crust

Bulk Pastry Mix (for pie crusts)

A good basic mix that will save you money each time you need a pie crust.

7 cups all-purpose flour
4 tsp. salt
1¾ cups solid vegetable shortening

In a large bowl, mix flour and salt. Cut in shortening with a pastry blender until mixture feels crumbly and is the size of tiny peas. Store in an airtight container in a cool, dry place.
Yields: about 6 pie crusts

Single Pie Crust

This is simple to make with the Bulk Pastry Mix prepared in advance.

2½ oz. water
1½ cups Bulk Pastry Mix (see recipe)

In a bowl, gradually add water to mix, blending until dough is smooth and workable. More water may be added by droplets, if needed, to make dough soft and pliable. Roll out on a lightly floured board.
Yields: 1 pie crust

TART SHELL

These dainty little tarts are so inexpensive to make and can be served with a variety of fillings.

1½ cups all-purpose flour
½ cup butter, melted
4 tsp. sugar
½ tsp. salt
¾ tsp. vanilla extract
3 to 4 tbsp. water

Mix all ingredients together in a bowl. Add additional water, if needed, to form a workable and smooth dough. Roll out on a floured board. Mold dough into cupcake tins and bake in a moderate oven until lightly browned. Remove tart shells from tins and cool before filling.

YIELDS: about 12 shells

CRÊPES

Try these delicious crêpes with fresh fruit and cream cheese filling.

1 cup all-purpose flour
2 eggs
1 tsp. vanilla extract
¼ tsp. salt
1 tsp. sugar
1¼ cups milk
2 tbsp. butter, melted

Combine all ingredients in an electric blender and beat on high until smooth. If mixing by hand, beat until smooth and mixture is free of lumps. Pour about 2 tbsp. of mixture into a hot, oiled shallow skillet. Tilt skillet to evenly distribute batter. Cook on both sides until browned. Remove from pan. Place on a towel to keep warm. Fill with meats, cheeses, creams, or fruits.

YIELDS: about 4 crêpes

Basic Sopaipilla Mix

It takes less time to make sopaipillas when you already have this basic mix ready.

7 cups all-purpose flour
4 tbsp. sugar
8 tsp. baking powder
4 tsp. salt
¼ cup solid vegetable shortening

In a mixing bowl, sift flour, sugar, baking powder, and salt. Cut in shortening with a pastry blender until mixture is crumbly like tiny peas. Store in an airtight container in a cool, dry place. Use to make Sopaipillas.
Yields: 7 cups

Sopaipillas

This treat is delicious with honey! Buy honey in a bottle with a pointed top and squeeze directly into the sopaipillas.

2 cups Basic Sopaipilla Mix (see recipe)
⅔ cup water
Vegetable oil

In a mixing bowl, combine mix and water. Knead dough until smooth. Roll out onto a lightly floured board to ¼" thick. Cut into 3" squares. Let rise 20 minutes in a warm place. Deep fry in hot oil. Drain on absorbent towels.
Yields: about 8 to 10 sopaipillas

VANILLA WAFERS
Great with a tall glass of ice-cold milk.

¾ cup sugar
1½ sticks butter, softened
2 tsp. vanilla extract
¼ tsp. almond extract
3 egg whites
½ tsp. salt
1⅓ cups cake flour

In a mixer, beat on high speed the sugar, butter, and vanilla and almond extracts until mixture is creamy and well blended. Add egg whites gradually and continue to beat. Sift salt and flour and mix with other ingredients to a smooth texture. Fill pastry bag using a wide, plain tube and pipe flattened rounds on greased cookie sheets. Bake in a 375-degree oven for about 12 to 15 minutes or until done.
YIELDS: about 15 wafers

BASIC BROWNIE MIX

6 cups all-purpose flour
4 tsp. baking powder
4 tsp. salt
8 cups sugar
1 8-oz. can unsweetened cocoa
2 cups solid vegetable shortening

Combine all dry ingredients together and sift twice. Cut in shortening with a pastry blender until dry mixture has the appearance of tiny peas. Store in an airtight container in a cool, dry place.
YIELDS: about 14 cups

BROWNIES

A deliciously moist brownie that is rich in taste.

2½ cups Basic Brownie Mix (see recipe)
2 eggs, beaten
1 tsp. vanilla extract
½ cup chopped walnuts or pecans

Thoroughly blend mix, eggs, and vanilla together until smooth. Stir in nuts. Pour batter into greased and floured pans. Bake in a 350-degree oven for about 30 minutes or until edges separate from pan. Let cool. Top with Chocolate Frosting (see recipe).
YIELDS: about 15 brownies

BASIC COOKIE MIX

Keep this bulk mix in your pantry and save time making your next batch of cookies.

9 cups all-purposes flour
3 cups nonfat dry milk (optional)
3 tbsp. baking powder
1 tbsp. salt
4 cups sugar
4 cups solid vegetable shortening

Mix together flour, dry milk (optional), baking powder, salt, and sugar. Cut in shortening with a pastry blender until mixture resembles tiny peas. Store in an airtight container in a cool, dry place.
YIELDS: about 14 cups

Basic Cookies

Change the taste of these delicious cookies by using different extracts, such as lemon, almond, or mint.

2 cups Basic Cookie Mix (see recipe)
1 egg
1 tbsp. vanilla extract

Mix all ingredients together until well blended. Form into dough. Roll or drop by teaspoonfuls on ungreased cookie sheets. Bake in a 350-degree oven for about 10 to 12 minutes or until lightly browned.

Yields: about 15 cookies

Basic Gingerbread Cookie Mix

Nothing but the best goes into this homemade mix, and it is cheaper than the name brands.

2 cups all-purpose flour
½ cup sugar
½ tsp. salt
1 tsp. baking powder
½ tsp. baking soda
1½ tsp. cinnamon
1 tsp. ground cloves
1 tsp. ginger
½ tsp. nutmeg
½ cup solid vegetable shortening

Sift all ingredients together except shortening. Cut shortening into the dry mix with pastry blender until mixture resembles tiny peas. Store in an airtight container or zip-type bag in a cool, dry place.

Yields: 1 packet

GINGERBREAD COOKIES

Cookies this good need to be made into gingerbread men.

1 packet Basic Gingerbread Cookie Mix (see recipe)
½ cup molasses
1 egg yolk

Thoroughly mix all ingredients together until well blended. Roll out on a lightly floured board to ¼" thickness. Cut into shapes with a cookie cutter (dusted with flour). Bake on ungreased cookie sheets at 350 degrees for about 8 to 10 minutes or until lightly browned.

YIELDS: about 15 cookies

BASIC GINGER SNAPS MIX

1 cup brown sugar
2¼ cup all-purpose flour
2 tsp. baking soda
½ tsp. salt
1 tsp. ground ginger
1 tsp. ground cinnamon
½ tsp. ground cloves
¾ cup solid vegetable shortening

Sift all ingredients together except shortening. Cut in shortening with pastry blender until mixture remembles tiny peas. Store in an airtight package in a cool, dry place.

YIELDS: 1 packet

GINGER SNAPS

This cookie matches perfectly with a cup of hot chocolate by the fireplace.

1 egg
¼ cup molasses
1 packet Ginger Snaps Basic Mix (see recipe)

Thoroughly mix all ingredients until well blended. Form into small balls. Roll in granulated sugar. Place 2" apart on greased cookie sheets. Bake in a 375-degree oven for about 10 to 12 minutes or until lightly browned.

YIELDS: about 4 dozen cookies

BASIC OATMEAL COOKIE MIX

You'll save a lot of money when you make this in bulk supply for your pantry.

3 cups all-purpose flour
2 tsp. baking soda
2 tsp. salt
2 cups sugar
2 cups brown sugar
2 cups solid vegetable shortening
6 cups quick oats, uncooked

Sift the first 5 ingredients together. Cut in shortening until mixture feels crumbly and has appearance of tiny peas. Add oats and mix until well blended. Store in an airtight container in a cool, dry place.

YIELDS: almost 12 cups

Oatmeal Cookies

4 cups Basic Oatmeal Cookie Mix (see recipe)
2 eggs, beaten
1 tbsp. water
2 tsp. vanilla extract
½ tsp. almond extract

Mix all ingredients until well blended. Grease cookie sheets. Drop batter by spoonfuls or shape in rounds. Bake in a 350-degree oven for about 10 to 12 minutes or until done.
YIELDS: about 2 dozen cookies

Hot Fudge Sauce

An excellent sauce to pour over ice cream.

6 tbsp. butter
6 squares unsweetened baking chocolate bar
1½ tsp. vanilla extract
½ cup light corn syrup
2 cups sugar

Melt butter and chocolate in a double boiler or use a microwave. Add remaining ingredients and blend well. Bring mixture to a boil over medium heat stirring constantly. Continue to cook until smooth and thick.
YIELDS: about 2½ cups

CHOCOLATE SYRUP

A delightfully sweet syrup to use in milk and ice cream.

½ cup unsweetened cocoa powder
1 cup water
2 cups sugar
⅛ tsp. salt
1 tsp. vanilla extract

In a saucepan, blend cocoa and water on medium to high heat. Add sugar and stir to dissolve. Reduce heat and allow to boil for only 1 minute, stirring to prevent sticking. Remove from heat and blend in salt and vanilla extract. When cool, the syrup will become thicker. Keep refrigerated.

YIELDS: about 2 cups

CHOCOLATE FROSTING

Cheaper than store bought and with no artificial fillers.

6 tbsp. butter
4 tbsp. powdered cocoa
3 tbsp. milk
Confectioners' sugar
1 tsp. vanilla extract

Melt butter in a small saucepan. Add cocoa. Then stir in milk and add enough confectioners' sugar to make a spreadable consistency. Add vanilla.

YIELDS: enough to frost an 8"x8" sheet cake

CHOCOLATE GLAZE
Try this glaze as a dip for strawberries.

3 oz. semisweet chocolate
2 tsp. butter

In a saucepan, melt the chocolate and butter or use a double boiler. Stir rapidly to blend and prevent mixture from sticking.
YIELDS: enough to dip 6 to 8 strawberries

HONEY FROSTING
Finally, a frosting for honey lovers!

3 tbsp. butter, softened
3 tbsp. cocoa powder
¾ tsp. vanilla extract
1 cup confectioners' sugar
1 tbsp. milk
1 tbsp. honey

In a small bowl, cream together butter and cocoa powder. Add vanilla and sugar. Blend in milk and honey and beat mixture until frosting is spreadable.
YIELDS: almost 1 cup

IRISH CRÈME FROSTING

¾ cup heavy cream
1½ tbsp. confectioners' sugar
1½ tsp. Irish whiskey
¼ tsp. instant coffee

In a chilled bowl with chilled mixer blades, beat cream and sugar, gradually adding whiskey and instant coffee powder until stiff peaks form.
YIELDS: almost 1 cup

CRÈME DE MENTHE FROSTING

2 cups confectioners' sugar
½ cup margarine
3 tbsp. crème de menthe liqueur

Mix all ingredients together until creamy.
YIELDS: almost ¾ cup

LEMON FROSTING

¼ cup butter
1 oz. unsweetened chocolate
2 cups or more confectioners' sugar
1 egg
1½ tsp. vanilla extract
1½ tsp. concentrated lemon juice

In a double boiler over simmering water, melt butter and chocolate. Add sugar and mix well. Blend in egg, vanilla, and lemon juice and stir until smooth. To thicken frosting, add more confectioners' sugar and mix well.
YIELDS: almost ¾ cup

CHOCOLATE-AMARETTO FROSTING

3 tbsp. butter, softened
1½ cups confectioners' sugar
4½ tsp. amaretto liqueur
4½ tsp. unsweetened cocoa powder
4½ tsp. hot coffee

Blend all ingredients together and beat until smooth. Blend in more confectioners' sugar if frosting needs to be thicker.
YIELDS: about ½ cup

WHITE ALMOND ICING

1 cup sifted confectioners' sugar
¼ tsp. almond extract
2 tbsp. half-and-half

In a bowl, mix sugar and almond extract. Add half-and-half a little at a time, mixing until creamy. Add more confectioners' sugar if mixture is too thin or more cream if mixture is too thick.
YIELDS: about ½ cup

CINNAMON GLAZE
A bakery-quality glaze to finish off your cinnamon rolls.

1 cup confectioners' sugar
2 to 4 tbsp. milk
¼ tsp. vanilla extract

In a small mixing bowl, combine confectioners' sugar and extract and add small amounts of milk to obtain a spreadable consistency. (Adjust amount of milk for proper consistency.)
YIELDS: about ½ cup

BASIC ANGEL FOOD CAKE MIX

1 cup cake flour
1½ cups sugar
1 tsp. cream of tartar
¼ tsp. salt

Combine all ingredients and sift 3 times. Store in an airtight container or zip-type bag in a cool, dry place. Use in Angel Food Cake recipe.
YIELDS: 1 packet

ANGEL FOOD CAKE

Keep strawberries and whipped cream on hand to partner with this fabulous cake.

1½ cups (about 12 eggs) egg whites
2½ tbsp. water
1 packet Basic Angel Food Cake Mix (see recipe)
½ tsp. vanilla extract
½ tsp. almond extract

In a mixing bowl, beat egg whites and water until stiff peaks form. Gradually fold in Basic Angel Food Cake Mix. Add vanilla and almond extracts and continue to beat until well blended. Bake in a greased and floured bundt pan at 350 degrees for about 50 minutes or until done.

BASIC CHOCOLATE CAKE MIX

Add this mix when making chocolate cake.

2 cups cake flour
⅔ cup unsweetened cocoa
1 tsp. baking soda
¾ tsp. salt
1½ cups sugar
⅔ cup solid vegetable shortening

In a large mixing bowl, sift all dry ingredients together. Cut in shortening with pastry blender until mixture feels crumbly. Store in an airtight zip-type bag. Label and date.
YIELDS: 1 packet

CHOCOLATE CAKE

Serve this scrumptious cake drenched with chocolate syrup and topped with shaved chocolate.

1 packet Basic Chocolate Cake Mix (see recipe)
1¼ cups milk
1 tsp. vanilla extract
2 eggs, beaten

In a large mixing bowl, combine cake mix, milk, and vanilla extract. Beat 2 minutes on high speed with an electric mixer and then add eggs. Continue to beat until thoroughly blended and smooth. Pour batter into a greased and floured pan and bake in a 350-degree oven for about 30 minutes or until done.

Basic Devil's Food Cake Mix

Use this basic mix with the Devil's Food Cake recipe. It will save you so much time.

2 cups sugar
1¾ cups all-purpose flour
¾ cup unsweetened cocoa
1½ tsp. baking soda
¾ tsp. salt
½ cup solid vegetable shortening

In a mixing bowl, sift all dry ingredients together. Cut in shortening with pastry blender until mixture feels crumbly. Store in an airtight zip-type bag in a cool, dry place. Label and date.
Yields: 1 packet

Devil's Food Cake

Add chocolate chips to the final mix before baking for that extra-rich chocolate taste.

1 packet Basic Devil's Food Cake Mix (see recipe)
1 tsp. vanilla extract
1⅔ cups milk
3 eggs, beaten

In a large mixing bowl, combine cake mix with vanilla extract and milk. Blend well. Add eggs and beat about 2 minutes on high speed in an electric mixer until smooth. Pour into a greased and floured pan. Bake at 350 degrees for about 30 to 35 minutes or until done.

POUND CAKE

You can make this rich pound cake for about half of what it costs at the store.

12 large eggs, separated
2 tsp. vanilla extract
1 tsp. lemon extract
2 cups butter
2 cups sugar
4 cups all-purpose flour
2 tsp. baking powder

In a bowl, beat egg yolks. Add vanilla and lemon extracts. In a large mixing bowl, cream butter and sugar until light. Add egg yolk mixture. Beat well with an electric mixer. In a separate bowl, sift flour and baking powder together and gradually add this to creamed mixture. Beat until thoroughly blended. Beat egg whites in a mixing bowl with an electric mixer until stiff. Fold into cake batter and hand mix until well blended. Pour into greased and floured loaf pans. Bake in a 350 degree oven for about 1 hour or until done.

YIELDS: 2 cakes

BASIC SPICE CAKE MIX

1 packet Basic Yellow Cake Mix (see recipe)
¼ cup sugar
1 tsp. cinnamon
½ tsp. ground cloves
¼ tsp. allspice

In a bowl, mix all ingredients together. Store in an airtight zip-type bag in a cool, dry place. Label and date.

YIELDS: 1 packet

SPICE CAKE

Hmmm. Smell the aroma of those sweet spices coming from your oven.

1 packet Basic Spice Cake Mix (see recipe)
¾ cup milk
2 eggs, well beaten

In an electric mixer, beat cake mix and milk on high speed for about 2 minutes. Add eggs and continue to beat until thoroughly blended and smooth. Grease and flour a pan. Pour mixture into pan and bake in a 350-degree oven for about 25 minutes or until done.

BASIC YELLOW CAKE MIX

Share a package or two of this wonderful mix with your friends.

2 cups cake flour
2½ tsp. baking powder
1 tsp. salt
1¼ cups sugar
½ cup solid vegetable shortening

In a large bowl, sift the cake flour, baking powder, salt, and sugar 3 times. Cut in shortening with pastry blender until mixture is crumbly and resembles small peas. Store in an airtight container in a cool, dry place. Date and label. Use this packet to make Yellow Cake and Spice Cake.
YIELDS: 1 packet

YELLOW CAKE

Tastes deliciously homemade.

1 packet Basic Yellow Cake Mix (see recipe)
¾ cup milk
1¼ tsp. vanilla extract
2 eggs, beaten

In a mixing bowl, combine cake mix, milk, and vanilla extract and beat with electric mixer on high speed for 2 minutes. Add eggs and continue to beat until mixture is well blended. Pour into a greased and floured pan. Bake in a 350-degree oven for about 25 minutes or until done.

BEVERAGES

TOMATO JUICE

18 fresh, ripe tomatoes
¾ cup water
1 tsp. celery salt
½ small onion
½ to ¾ tsp. sugar
1 tbsp. lemon juice

Combine all ingredients in an electric blender. Blend on high speed until puréed. Strain using a sieve. Discard any pulp. Store in a covered container in refrigerator. Shake before each use. Serve cold.
YIELDS: 8 servings

VEGETABLE 8 JUICE

6 carrots, peeled
1 14.5-oz. can diced tomatoes
3 stalks celery
1 small bell pepper
¼ sweet onion
1 small beet
Handful of spinach, stems removed
Handful of cabbage or lettuce leaves
Salt

Wash all vegetables thoroughly and process through a juicing machine. Add salt to taste.
YIELDS: about 24 oz.

CRANBERRY JUICE

1 can jellied cranberry sauce
2 tbsp. lemon juice
1 qt. water
¾ cup sugar
1 qt. apple juice

Using an electric blender, process on highest speed cranberry sauce, lemon juice, 2 cups water, and sugar until completely dissolved and well blended. Remove to larger container and add apple juice and balance of water. Mix thoroughly. Refrigerate. Best when served cold.

YIELDS: ½ gallon

GRAPE JUICE

Fresh concord grapes

Clean and wash grapes. Place in a pot with very little water and bring to a boil, or heat until pulp separates from seeds. Stir often. Put through a sieve to remove pulp and seeds from juice. Per 1 qt. of juice add 1¼ cups sugar and 2 cups of water. Keep refrigerated.

Fruit Punch

5 cups sugar
12 cups water
1 46-oz. can pineapple juice
4½ cups orange juice
1½ cups lemon juice concentrate
3 qt. ginger ale (optional)

Combine all ingredients except the ginger ale in a large container. Add ginger ale to the container right before serving. Stir.
Yields: 9 qt.

Hot Cocoa Mix

1 cup powdered, nondairy coffee creamer
2 cups powdered, nonfat dry milk
¾ cup unsweetened cocoa powder
1 cup sugar

In a large bowl, sift together coffee creamer, dry milk, and cocoa powder 3 times. Stir in sugar and blend well. Store in an airtight container in a cool, dry place.
Yields: about 4¾ cups

Hot Cocoa

⅓ cup Hot Cocoa Mix (see recipe)
¼ tsp. vanilla extract
Dash of cinnamon or allspice
8 oz. boiling water

Add cocoa mix, vanilla, and a dash of cinnamon to a cup. Stir in just enough boiling water to form a smooth paste. Add balance of water. Stir to blend well.

Yields: 1 cup

Instant Breakfast in a Glass

1 banana, sliced
⅓ cup milk
1½ tbsp. frozen orange juice concentrate, undiluted
1 tsp. wheat germ
1 6-oz. container banana-strawberry yogurt
2 tsp. honey

Place all ingredients in an electric blender and whip at high speed for 1 minute or until liquified. Pour into a cold glass.

Yields: 1 serving

LEMONADE SYRUP CONCENTRATE

3 cups sugar
1 cup water
1 tbsp. grated lemon peel
3 cups lemon juice
2 tsp. honey

In a saucepan, heat to a boil sugar and water until sugar is dissolved. Add lemon peel, lemon juice, and honey. Stir to blend. Refrigerate in a closed container. To make instant lemonade, add ⅓ cup Lemonade Syrup Concentrate to ¾ cup ice water. Stir and serve.
YIELDS: about 15 cups

ORANGE SMOOTHIE

⅓ cup frozen orange juice concentrate, undiluted
⅓ cup sugar or honey
½ cup milk
⅓ cup water
½ tsp. vanilla extra
6 to 8 ice cubes

Place all ingredients in an electric blender and blend on high until ice is crushed. Pour and serve in frosted glasses.
YIELDS: about 2 servings

Ice Cream Soda

1 cup sugar
1 envelope unsweetened soft drink mix (any flavor)
1 cup water
1 28-oz. bottle club soda
1 pt. vanilla ice cream

In a large glass or plastic bowl or pitcher, dissolve sugar and unsweetened soft drink mix with water. (Do not use metal bowl or metal pitcher.) Add club soda and stir to blend. Place a scoop of ice cream in a glass and add liquid mixture. Top with additional scoop of ice cream. Add whipped topping and cherries, if desired.
YIELDS: 4 to 6 servings

Egg Nog

6 eggs
⅔ cup sugar
⅛ tsp. salt
2 tbsp. vanilla extract
¼ tsp. ground cloves
¼ tsp. ground nutmeg
2 tsp. ground cinnamon
2 cups whole milk
2 12-oz. cans evaporated milk
Rum to taste (optional)

Place eggs, sugar, spices, and 2 cups milk in container of electric blender. Blend on high speed until thoroughly mixed. Pour into a large pot and add remaining milk. Heat, stirring constantly. Add rum per cup or to taste. Serve hot with cinnamon sticks in cups for stirring.
YIELDS: 1½ qt.

Café Orleans Mix

1½ cups powdered, extra-rich coffee creamer
½ cup firmly packed brown sugar
½ cup instant coffee, regular or decaffeinated

In a food processor or electric blender, combine all dry ingredients and blend into a powder. Store in an airtight container.
Yields: enough for 6 servings

Café Orleans

⅓ cup Café Orleans Mix
⅔ cup boiling water
Kahlúa

Add mix to boiling water and stir in ¼ to ½ tsp. Kahlúa per cup or to taste.
Yields: 1 serving

Café Vienna Mix

1 cup instant coffee
1⅓ cups sugar
¾ cup nonfat dry milk
¾ cup powdered, nondairy coffee creamer
¼ cup unsweetened cocoa powder
1 tsp. cinnamon
Dash of nutmeg
Dash of cloves (optional)

Combine all ingredients in a bowl. Sift ½ cup at a time until powdery. Return completed mix to a large bowl and whisk to blend mixture. Store in an airtight container.
Yields: about 4 cups

CAFÉ VIENNA

1½ heaping tbsp. Café Vienna Mix (see recipe)
1 cup boiling water

Add mix to 1 cup of boiling water. Stir well. Add more or less Café Vienna. Mix to taste.
YIELDS: 1 serving

ALMOND-FLAVORED COFFEE CREAMER

1 tsp. almond extract
1 cup powdered, nondairy coffee creamer

Add extract and creamer to food processor and process on high until thoroughly blended. Store in an airtight container in a cool, dry place.

NONFOODS

CRAYON DISCS

Broken pieces of crayons
Midget foil baking cups

Gather all broken crayons and remove paper. Break into very small pieces and place in foil-lined baking cups. Crayons may be sorted by color or combined for unusual colored creations. Heat oven to 500 degrees and bake cups in oven for about 5 minutes or until melted. Remove from oven. Crayons will harden when cooled. **Caution:** These beautiful crayon discs are perfect for those little fingers, but they also look yummy. Children should be supervised, as these are not edible.

BABY POWDER EXTENDER

Cornstarch is all-natural and adds much needed absorbency to baby powder.

1 14-oz. box baby powder
1 16-oz. box cornstarch

Mix baby powder with cornstarch until well blended. Add mixture to baby powder container.

BATH POWDER

This powder is a real money saver over the store-bought products. Vary the oils for a lively selection of bath powders.

2 cups cornstarch
8 drops oil of rose or lavender

Thoroughly combine all ingredients with a wire whisk. Store in a shaker bottle or use in a closed container as a dusting powder.

BATH SALTS

A hot soothing bath awaits you with these specially blended bath salts.

3 cups Epsom Salt
1 cup table salt
2 cups baking soda
Infused oil of your choice

Mix salts and baking soda in a large bowl. Add essential oil until desired scent is obtained. Bath salts should have a strong scent. Place the bath salt mixture in a container with a tight-fitting lid and shake well before each use.

DENTAL FLOSS

This is a real money saver. Instead of buying floss from the store, substitute white quilter's thread for dental floss and pocket the cash. Besides, you get so much more with a spool of quilter's thread than the brand-name floss.

DENTURE CLEANER

Hydrogen peroxide is an inexpensive whitener. You are sure to save money using this recipe.

½ cup hydrogen peroxide, 3 percent
½ cup water

Combine hydrogen peroxide with water in a bowl. Soak dentures in this solution overnight. Rinse and use.

DEODORANT

Pat baking soda under arms after showering. The body should be slightly damp but not wet. If baking soda is too abrasive, mix with cornstarch. Discontinue use if irritation occurs.

SHAMPOO

This fortifying shampoo nourishes the hair.

1 oz. olive oil
1 egg, beaten
1 tbsp. lemon juice
½ tsp. apple cider vinegar

Combine all ingredients in a mixing bowl. Beat until well blended. Use as you would any shampoo.

Lip Balm and Gloss

An all-natural lip gloss and balm that nourishes and heals the skin.

1 tsp. aloe vera gel
1 tsp. petroleum jelly
½ tsp. coconut oil

Combine all ingredients in a microwave-safe bowl. Heat about 1 minute. Remove from heat. Stir and pour into a small container. Cool before using.

Facial Exfoliator

With this all-natural formula, you'll have nature's best.

2 tsp. ground oatmeal
1 tsp. baking soda
Water

Combine ground oatmeal with baking soda. Add just enough water to form a paste. Apply to skin and rub gently. Rinse and gently pat dry.

Oatmeal-and-Honey Facial Mask

This all-natural facial mask does not contain any colorings, chemicals, or mystery additives.

½ cup oatmeal
2 tbsp. honey

Blend oatmeal and honey together. Apply on face and leave on for 30 minutes. Rinse and pat dry.

Facial Cleaning Pads

No make-up removers to buy just use baby wipes. They are easier to use and save you money.

Baby wipes

One baby wipe cut in quarters makes 4 cleaning pads. Use as you would a cotton pad. Not only does it clean, but it also moisturizes and conditions your skin.

Premoistened Towelettes

These can be made like the name brands but cost a lot less.

Baby oil
Heavy-quality, soft, absorbent paper towels

Cut each paper towel in half. Trifold each half. Place in a covered wide-mouth jar or other airtight container. Saturate with baby oil. Use as a quick wipe up for baby.

Foaming Liquid Hand Soap

10 oz. water
6 tbsp. liquid dishwashing soap
1 empty liquid hand pump container (preferably a
    Dawn Direct Foam Pump container)

Fill hand pump with water then add liquid dishwashing soap. I recommend that you buy the Dawn Direct Foam Pump because it is more durable and lasts much longer than the other liquid soap pumps. It also dispenses much better. If the dispenser bottle becomes clogged, fill the empty container with a bit of white vinegar and lots of water and pump it through the squirter. Your dispenser will work just fine after that.

DISHWASHER DETERGENT

You don't have to pay a lot for those little tablets. This works great.

2 tbsp. baking soda
2 tbsp. borax

Mix baking soda with borax. Use in your dishwasher.

DRY LAUNDRY DETERGENT

You will never run out of laundry detergent now that you have the formula.

1 cup grated soap
½ cup Arm & Hammer Washing Soda
½ cup Twenty Mule Team Borax

Mix all ingredients together. Store in an airtight container. This product contains no fillers, so you can use less. Start with ½ cup per small load.

LAUNDRY PRESOAK FOR WHITES ONLY

Your white clothes will look so much cleaner using this formula.

¾ cup automatic dishwasher detergent
2 gallons hot water
¾ cup bleach

Use caution and read label on automatic dishwasher detergent to see if bleach can be added to the detergent. Mix all ingredients in washing machine. Do not use on colored clothing. Soak whites in machine with presoak mixture. After no longer than 30 minutes, run clothes through the wash cycle.

STAIN REMOVER

1 qt. water
¼ cup vinegar
1 tbsp. laundry detergent, with no bleach
¼ cup household ammonia

In a well-ventilated room, mix water, vinegar, and detergent. Add ammonia. Store in a spray bottle. Spot treat stains, working in with a clean cloth. Spray again and soak overnight.

SPRAY STARCH

10 oz. water
1 tbsp. cornstarch

In a small jar, combine water and cornstarch. Tighten lid and shake well to dissolve cornstarch. Pour into a spray bottle to apply. Shake before each use. Add more cornstarch for heavier-starched clothing or more water for lighter-starched clothing.

DISINFECTING CLEANERS
Makes a great disinfectant especially for toilets and showers.

1 cup rubbing alcohol
1 cup household ammonia
1 spray bottle

Mix alcohol and ammonia and store in a spray bottle.

APPLIANCE CLEANER

This also makes a great polish and deodorizer for Formica and tile countertops.

1 cup white vinegar
1 cup household ammonia

In a well-ventilated room, mix both ingredients and pour into a spray bottle. This formula works well on chrome fixtures, too. Simply spray and wipe dry.

GARBAGE DISPOSAL CLEANER

Use this formula often to get rid of odors in your garbage disposal.

¾ cup baking soda
½ used lemon
1 cup white vinegar
1 gallon boiling water

With garbage disposal turned off, pour baking soda down the drain along with the lemon. Add vinegar. Allow mixture to foam for 5 minutes. Flush the drain with 1 gallon of boiling water. Turn on garbage disposal until drained.

LEMON-SCENTED FURNITURE POLISH

Condition your wood with this lemon-scented polish that costs far less than the brand name.

1 tsp. lemon oil
2 cups mineral oil

Mix and store in an airtight container. Apply to furniture with a soft cloth. Wipe off any excess with a soft, dry cloth.

Furniture Polish

The richness of olive oil will enhance the beauty of your wood.

½ cup olive oil
1 tbsp. lemon juice or white vinegar

Mix and store in an airtight container. Apply to furniture with a soft cloth. Wipe off any excess.

Glass Cleaner

This formula is the best I have ever found. Use fresh towels for streak-free windows.

1 cup household ammonia
1 cup white vinegar
½ cup rubbing alcohol

In a well-ventilated room, mix all ingredients together and store in a spray bottle.

Microwave Cleaner

1 cup water
1 tsp. liquid dishwashing detergent
1 tsp. white vinegar

Place all ingredients in a microwavable bowl. Set temperature on high for about 2 minutes so water will reach boiling stage. Let set a couple of minutes to allow steam to help loosen food splatters. Wipe off with a damp cloth. Stubborn stains may need additional treatments.

OIL OF ROSE

1 qt. safflower oil
Fresh rose petals

Pour safflower oil in a shallow pan and cover surface with rose petals, letting each one lightly overlap the other. After a couple of days, remove the old petals being careful not to remove any of the oil. Replace with fresh rose petals. Repeat the process a dozen times or so to obtain the desired strength. With each application of fresh petals, the scent becomes stronger. Pour oil in a tightly closed jar.

PLANT FOOD

1 tbsp. Epsom Salt
1 tsp. baking powder
1 tsp. salt
½ tsp. household ammonia
1 gallon water

In a well-ventilated room, add Epsom Salt, baking powder, salt, and ammonia to 1 gallon of water. Shake to mix. Use once a month as a fertilizer for plants.

Paste Wax

Adding paste wax to your furniture will bring out the beauty of your wood.

4½ oz. beeswax
1 cup turpentine or mineral spirits

Break up beeswax or grate. Heat wax in top of a double boiler until wax has melted. Blend with turpentine. Stir as necessary. Let the wax cool. It should be like softened butter for a workable texture. To thicken the wax, add more wax and reheat. To thin it, add more solvent and reheat.

Roach Killer

This really kills the roaches!

16 oz. boric acid powder
1 cup flour
¼ cup sugar
½ cup shortening
Water

Sift boric acid, flour, and sugar together. Cut in shortening with pastry blender. Add enough water to form a soft workable dough. Roll into small balls and place them throughout the house in hidden corners, behind cabinets, etc. **Caution:** This is a poison. Keep away from children and pets.

RUG DEODORIZER

Baking soda neutralizes odors and keeps your house smelling clean without using chemicals.

Baking soda
Sifter

Pour baking soda into sifter. Sift over the entire carpet. Vacuum as usual.

SCOURING POWDER

Great for use on pots and pans.

¼ cup borax
¼ cup baking soda
¼ cup table salt

Blend all ingredients in a bowl. Store in an airtight container.

SILVERWARE CLEANER

Pocket the cost of silver cleaners with this quick-and-easy way to keep your silver beautiful.

6 cups water
3 tsp. baking soda
1 tsp. salt
1 piece aluminum foil

In a large pot, combine water, soda, and salt and bring to a boil. Drop in aluminum foil to bottom of pot. Place silverware on top of foil and continue boiling for about 5 minutes. Remove from heat and retrieve silver. Wash and dry silver. Aluminum will turn black and silver will come out clean.

Windshield Washer Fluid

9 cups water
1 cup rubbing alcohol
1 tbsp. dishwashing liquid
Plastic jug

Place all ingredients in the jug and shake to blend. Use as washer fluid and in a spray bottle for cleaning windshields.

PETS

CHICKEN CAT FOOD

This formula contains a special blend of fresh ingredients to help keep your cat fit and healthy.

2 hard-boiled eggs
2 tbsp. cooked green beans
3 tbsp. cooked chicken
2 tbsp. cooked carrots
⅔ cup cooked rice (preferably brown rice)
2 tbsp. olive oil

With your food processor or using an electric blender, mix all ingredients to a soft consistency, adding a little extra olive oil if needed. Keep refrigerated in an airtight container. Use within 36 hours. Freezes well in a zip-type freezer bag or container.
YIELDS: about 2 cups

KITTY LITTER

You will never have to pay grocery-store prices again for your cat litter. It is practically free to make at home and a fantastic way to recycle those old newspapers, magazines, and even junk mail.

Line the litter pan with used plastic grocery bags before placing the shredded papers inside. This will make it easier to clean up. Shred newspapers, magazines, and junk mail in a paper shredder or cut into narrow strips, then soak the papers in a bowl of warm water containing a few squirts of mild dishwasher soap (no perfumes). This is to clean the paper of all ink. Drain in an old colander and repeat this process without using soap. Sprinkle baking soda generously over the wet paper. Using plastic gloves (this keeps from staining your hands), knead then squeeze out all of the remaining moisture until the paper is as dry as you can get it. The mixture will resemble cooked oatmeal. Using a screen, spread the paper mixture loosely and allow to dry thoroughly before using.

Puppy Treats

Tasty peanut butter will have your puppy jumping with excitement.

2 cups all-purpose flour
1 tbsp. baking powder
1 cup peanut butter
1 cup milk

Combine flour and baking powder in a separate bowl. Set aside. In another bowl, mix peanut butter and milk. Add dry ingredients and combine. Place dough on a floured surface and knead to ¼" thickness. Add more milk or flour to mix, if needed, to make dough more pliable. Cut out with cookie cutters. Bake on a greased and floured cookie sheet at 375 degrees for about 20 minutes or until lightly browned.

YIELDS: about 2 dozen treats

Doggie Bones

You will have fun creating bones from this dough.

¾ cup hot water
⅓ cup margarine
½ cup powdered milk
1 tsp. salt
1 egg, beaten
3 cups all-purpose flour

In a large saucepan, combine hot water with margarine. Stir in powdered milk, salt, and beaten egg. Gradually add flour and blend thoroughly. Knead to form a stiff dough, adding additional flour or milk as necessary. Roll out onto a floured board to ½" thickness. Cut into bone shapes. Bake on a greased and floured cookie sheet at 325 degrees for about 50 minutes or until done. Cool. Let dry out to harden.

YIELDS: about 2 dozen "bones"

Dog Cookies
Your dog will love these nutritious chicken-flavored cookies.

2 cups all-purpose flour
⅔ cup yellow cornmeal
2 eggs, beaten
¼ cup milk
2 tbsp. corn oil
½ cup chicken broth

In a large bowl, sift flour and cornmeal until blended. In a separate bowl, beat eggs and milk. Add to dry mixture along with oil and broth. Blend, adding additional milk or flour as needed to form a soft pliable dough. Shape into cookies or use cookie cutter. Bake in a 350-degree oven for about 25 to 30 minutes or until golden brown. Cool.
Yields: about 28 cookies

Flea Powder
This safe, all-natural flea powder is free of harsh chemicals.

2 tbsp. dried pennyroyal
2 tbsp. dried fennel
2 tbsp. cornstarch

Mix all ingredients together. Dust pet with powder by rubbing into skin. Make sure to dust pet bedding.

INDEX